Publisher's Message for
IRRESPONSIBLE GOVERNMENT

To shed light on today's cultural, social, economic, and political issues that are shaping our future as Canadians, Dundurn's **Point of View** books offer readers the informed opinions of knowledgeable individuals.

The author of a **Point of View** book is someone we've invited to address a vital topic because his or her front-line experience, arising from personal immersion in the issue, gives readers an engaging perspective, even though a reader may not ultimately reach all the same conclusions as the author.

Our publishing house is committed to framing the hard choices facing Canadians in a way that will spur democratic debate in our country. For over forty years, Dundurn has been "defining Canada for Canadians." Now our **Point of View** books, under the direction of general editor J. Patrick Boyer, take us a further step on this journey of national discovery.

Authors of **Point of View** books have an important message, and a definite point of view about an issue close to their hearts. Some **Point of View** books resemble manifestos for action, others shed light on a crucial subject from an alternative perspective, and a few are concise statements of a timely case needing to be clearly made.

But whatever the topic or whomever the author, all these titles are eye-openers for Canadians, engaging issues that matter to us as citizens.

J. Kirk Howard
President

A Note from the General Editor

In this first **Point of View** book, MP Brent Rathgeber uses the long lens of historical perspective to bring clarity to present day conundrums of "responsible government."

The constitutional provisions by which elected representatives of the people hold ministers of the Crown to account for their spending, policies, and programs became the cornerstone of our system of parliamentary government in the mid-1800s. The slow passage of time and the incremental concentration of power around prime ministers and provincial premiers, however, has seen this relationship become imbalanced, if not completely unhinged.

Last year, when the Alberta member of the House of Commons took issue with the way he, as an elected representative, was being manipulated by the Prime Minister's Office, he followed principle and resigned from the Conservative caucus to sit as an Independent parliamentarian. While party discipline has a necessary role, it was certainly refreshing to see some backbone on the backbench.

Now, in *Irresponsible Government,* Mr. Rathgeber shares with all Canadians just what those principles of responsible government mean today, and why they matter to us all.

J. Patrick Boyer
General Editor
Point of View books

IRRESPONSI
GOVERNME

IRRESPONSIBLE GOVERNMENT

THE DECLINE OF PARLIAMENTARY DEMOCRACY IN CANADA

BRENT RATHGEBER

FOREWORD BY ANDREW COYNE

DUNDURN

A J. PATRICK BOYER BOOK

TORONTO

Editor: Dominic Farrell
Design: Laura Boyle
Cover Design: Courtney Horner
Front Cover Image: © Veer/ Smit
Printer: Webcom

Library and Archives Canada Cataloguing in Publication

Rathgeber, Brent, 1964-, author
        Irresponsible government : the decline of parliamentary democracy in Canada / Brent Rathgeber; foreword by Andrew Coyne.

Issued in print and electronic formats.
ISBN 978-1-4597-2837-0 (pbk.).--ISBN 978-1-4597-2838-7 (pdf).
--ISBN 978-1-4597-2839-4 (epub)

1. Executive-legislative relations--Canada. 2. Representative government and representation--Canada. 3. Canada. Parliament--Powers and duties. 4. Canada--Politics and government--21st century. I. Title.

JL136.R37 2014   320.971'09051   C2014-904276-0
                                              C2014-904277-9

1 2 3 4 5   18 17 16 15 14

Conseil des Arts du Canada   Canada Council for the Arts   ONTARIO ARTS COUNCIL CONSEIL DES ARTS DE L'ONTARIO an Ontario government agency un organisme du gouvernement de l'Ontario

We acknowledge the support of the **Canada Council for the Arts** and the **Ontario Arts Council** for our publishing program. We also acknowledge the financial support of the **Government of Canada** through the **Canada Book Fund and Livres Canada Books**, and the **Government of Ontario** through the Ontario Book Publishing Tax Credit and the **Ontario Media Development Corporation**.

Care has been taken to trace the ownership of copyright material used in this book. The author and the publisher welcome any information enabling them to rectify any references or credits in subsequent editions.

J. Kirk Howard, President

The publisher is not responsible for websites or their content unless they are owned by the publisher.

Printed and bound in Canada.

Visit us at

Dundurn.com | @dundurnpress | Facebook.com/dundurnpress | Pinterest.com/dundurnpress

Dundurn
3 Church Street, Suite 500
Toronto, Ontario, Canada
M5E 1M2

This book is dedicated to my late father, Ernest, an educator, who taught me the value of civics — the rights, duties, and responsibilities of citizens — but who died long before I was able to practise his wisdom.

CONTENTS

FOREWORD

Until the 1930s, it was the convention and indeed the law in Canada that an MP, on appointment to Cabinet, had first to resign his seat and run in a by-election. The reason: his role had changed, from being a watchdog on the government to being a member of it. As such he was obliged to ask his electors' permission.

Contrast that to the present day. The idea of members of the governing party acting as any sort of effective check on the prime minister or Cabinet is so far removed from current practice that I doubt many Canadians could even imagine it. Nowadays, as Brent Rathgeber writes in this eloquent lament for what we have lost, they are more cheerleaders than watchdogs. They do not see their role as to hold government to account; indeed, they see themselves as part of it. They "show up at government funding announcements in their ridings," he writes, "often with oversized novelty cheques (sometimes bearing the party logo) bragging and taking credit for the pork that has just been delivered."

What we have lost, in short, is "responsible government," the great achievement of pre-Confederation Canada. Government is no longer responsible to Parliament in any meaningful way. Opposition MPs lack the tools, and government MPs lack the incentive, preferring to angle for one of the many scores of offices in the prime minister's power to bestow. "Canada," Rathgeber writes, "has had responsible government since 1848, and a constitution since 1867. The latter remains substantially unaltered; the former has been almost completely destroyed."

The critique is neither exaggerated nor new. Indeed, similar complaints have been heard for decades; what is new, however, is that the present government came to power promising to restore what previous governments had undermined. But Rathgeber is no ordinary critic. The decline of Parliament, the neutering of MPs, isn't an abstract complaint to him: as a Conservative MP, he lived it. He saw how the system has broken down close up, from the inside. And, exceptionally, he chose to do something about it, first by resigning from caucus in protest, and now with this book.

As he describes, nothing in our present system works as it is supposed to. The dominance of the executive over Parliament, and of party leaders over caucus, pervades everything, from how we nominate candidates to how we elect party leaders, from how elections are conducted to how Parliament works, or fails to. Other checks and balances — the media, the bureaucracy, the courts — are no substitute for a democratically elected Parliament, accountable to the people and as such in a unique position to demand accountability from government.

Notably, Rathgeber makes clear the real-world consequences of this, such as the decades-long failure of Parliament to control public spending, or, in the extreme, scandals like the Wright-Duffy affair, in which a sitting legislator was paid tens of thousands of dollars to keep quiet about a matter embarrassing to the government: the logical consequence of a system where all power resides in the Prime Minister's Office.

"Irresponsible government," he writes, "has not served Canadians well." But before they can be persuaded to demand change, "the electorate will need to be convinced that reform is in their best interest in a tangible way, not merely at a conceptual level."

Rathgeber offers several recommendations for reform. Of these, the most intriguing is his suggestion that members of Cabinet be appointed from outside Parliament — a hybrid of the American and Canadian systems, in which the government would be accountable to the Commons but not of it. If MPs had no possibility of becoming ministers, he reasons, they would be less inclined to servility, more inclined to perform the watchdog role as of old. I am reflexively hostile — smaller cabinets would achieve much the same purpose, surely — but the idea can't be dismissed outright.

And certainly any would-be reformers would do well to start with the analysis offered in these pages: as clear-eyed as it is forthright, a passionate call to arms, for a democracy in need of defenders.

Andrew Coyne *is a columnist with Postmedia; his columns appear in the* National Post, *the* Ottawa Citizen, *and other papers in the chain. His writing has also appeared in* Maclean's, *Saturday Night, the* Globe and Mail, *the* New York Times, *the* Wall Street Journal, *and* Time. *Coyne appears frequently as a commentator on television political affairs programs, including the "At Issue" panel on CBC's* The National.

INTRODUCTION

On June 5, 2013, I resigned from the Conservative caucus of the Canadian House of Commons. I was elected as the Conservative MP for Edmonton-St. Albert in October 2008 and re-elected in May of 2011. Prior to my election to Parliament, I had served one term in the Alberta Legislature, and for a little more than a decade before that I was a trial lawyer. I have also worked inside government, mostly during my university years, most notably as an executive assistant to a Saskatchewan cabinet minister. I have also been employed as a student employment counsellor and as a research officer for the Public Prosecutions Branch and Labour Relations Board of the Government of Saskatchewan.

I am a conservative. Accordingly, I have an inherent mistrust of government and government institutions. I believe that government is necessary, as there are many projects and public works that can only be achieved effectively as a collective. However, I believe said projects are fewer than are commonly believed. Although government is necessary, I continue to believe that the government that governs least governs best.

As a result, I believe that modern governments at all levels have grown too big, have attempted to do too much, and have grown too expensive. Social engineering and well-intentioned attempts at improving the human condition have led to a "government knows best" philosophy guiding the modern nanny state.

Although attempts at reducing poverty and income disparity are both laudable and have, to some extent, been successful, many other government initiatives and programs are neither. The result is government institutions that consume greater and greater portions of private resources, while simultaneously digging themselves deeper and deeper into debt. For a hundred years, the Government of Canada could generally pay its bills as they came due. However, the modern welfare state, with its requirement for greater program spending and an expensive bureaucracy for administering its universal social programs, has burdened Canada with more than $600 billion of debt.

Provinces, including my home province, resource rich Alberta, now routinely run deficits. Even municipalities have gotten into the debt financing business. My home, located in Edmonton, will see its property taxes increase by 5 percent this year, while the city pays off a $2.2 billion debt.[1] This is occurring while municipal infrastructure, primarily roads and bridges, continues to deteriorate.

Meanwhile, Canadians continue to pay taxes in ever increasing amounts. Taxes continue to absorb over 40 percent of the average Canadian's salary.[2] Worse, when one level of government lowers one tax or another, another level of government will happily fill the newly created gap.

These practices are not sustainable. The myth that a government can continue to spend in excess of its revenue has been dispelled. Welfare states such as Greece, Portugal, and Spain have all had to renegotiate their debt loads and have had to implement extreme austerity measures as a condition for refinancing. Closer to home, the City of Detroit has actually applied for bankruptcy protection from its creditors. Yes, a city on the Canadian border has petitioned for bankruptcy! Detroit, a city smaller than Edmonton, is carrying a debt load more than nine times that of Edmonton and can no longer pay its bills as they come due.

Many Canadian cities face money challenges; but, I know of none that have similar solvency challenges. However, government debt is an issue at every level. The Government of Canada, for example, currently allocates eleven cents of every tax dollar toward interest.[3] Federal income taxes could be reduced, or, alternatively, program spending could be increased, by 11 percent if governments over the last half-century had exercised more fiscal discipline. Meanwhile, municipalities, such as my hometown of Edmonton, spend upward of 13 percent of tax revenue collected on debt repayment.[4] Only the money allocated to the police service ranks higher than interest charges on the Edmonton Expenditure Statement,[5] a sobering fact that I reflect on every time I drive into a pothole.

So, how did we get into this mess? Stated simply, our elected officials have failed in their duty to be good stewards over the public purse. Government institutions, by their very nature, will attempt to grow both in scope and size; it is incumbent, therefore, on legislatures and municipal councils to provide a check on such institutions' attempts at expansive growth.

It is not realistic to expect civil servants, at any level, to exercise fiscal discipline. In a culture where bureaucratic success and influence is measured by growth in the mandarin's budget and the number of employees supervised, it is the job of elected representatives to defend taxpayers against unsustainable government growth. Many of the projects promoted by government, either by the bureaucratic social engineers or their political masters, are, of course, positive and laudable — the issue is whether or not they are affordable.

Affordability is both subjective and conditional on revenue, though the latter concept seems lost on institutions that are paying for projects with someone else's money. Individuals and families, however, understand these concepts intuitively at the micro level. Every household understands that although one can purchase a home by taking out a mortgage one cannot live forever on borrowed funds.

The same family also understands that one cannot consistently use high-interest credit cards to pay for unnecessary, though perhaps desirable, consumer goods such as big screen televisions and exotic winter vacations. As long as the household is able to make the interest payments on its credit card debt, it will be like Canada: spending too much of its income on interest, and, therefore, reducing its actual purchasing power in the process. When the household ceases to be able to pay the required minimums, however, it becomes more like Detroit: insolvent.

Insolvency throws everything into disarray. In the case of personal bankruptcy, assets are surrendered, budgets are imposed, and creditors, some who might be personally known to the bankrupt, are left bitter and holding the bag. In the case of a government, like Detroit, becoming insolvent, the jobs and the vested pensions of public employees are threatened and all programs and services are jeopardized, whether necessary or not.

In the language of governmental budgeting, words like "desirable" and "necessary" have become synonymous; they are not. More troubling still, questions of affordability seem to become irrelevant once a project is deemed to be necessary, or even merely desirable.

It is not reasonable to expect a child to appreciate the difference between necessary and desirable (a child will still want to go to Disneyland notwithstanding the fact that his mother has just had her employment hours reduced); however, government bureaucrats should be able to make the distinction. The fact that they seem unable to may arise from the fact that the projects are being funded with public money rather than their own resources.

This concept is central to the principle of financial accountability — the person making the financial decisions, ideally, should be the one who is responsible for paying the tab. Since the child does not pay the bills in most households, he will generally not be able to distinguish between something that is a necessity, like school supplies or prescription medication, and something that is merely desirable, like a trip to Disneyland or a new Xbox.

Like the child, civil servants will often evaluate projects based on their desirability rather than their necessity or even their affordability. This is natural since they do not personally have to pay for the project themselves. But somebody does have to pay for these projects, and in the case of public works and government programs and services, that somebody is the taxpayer. Accordingly, if elected representatives do not keep an eye on public spending, public spending will go unchecked.

❖

Every four years or so, the taxpayers elect a group of peers to represent them at the respective levels of government. The expectation is that the elected officials will provide representation; that they will pass appropriate laws and that they will hold government to account. The bureaucracy (i.e., the permanent government) does not represent taxpayers; their job is to design and administer government programs and services. It is the elected Parliament, legislatures, and municipal councils who must represent taxpayers if taxpayers are to be represented; it is the elected bodies that must hold government to account. Failing that, government will by definition become unaccountable.

As I will show in the following chapters, the people's elected representatives in Canada have failed miserably in their constitutional duty to hold government to account. This is true for all levels of government. At the federal level, consolidation of power, first in the cabinet and more recently in the Prime Minister's Office, has not only led to a diminished role for Parliament in both the budgetary and legislative processes, but also to the predictable growth in governments' size and expense. Even "conservative" governments cannot resist the institution's natural tendency toward expansion. Alongside of this, there has been a parallel growth in the government's consolidation of power — something that has occurred at the expense of Parliament and its members. Ironically, the current executive's attempts at neutering the legislative branch, including its own caucus, challenge its very claim to being conservative.

My decision to resign from the caucus of the governing Conservative Party was widely reported to be a result of the government's deliberate decision to eviscerate my private member's bill dealing with disclosure and transparency of public servant salaries, responsibilities, and expenses. Although this is true, my action was not motivated by private feelings of disappointment; rather, I resigned because I came to realize that the gutting was indicative of a more general lack of commitment to transparency and open government. Values that brought me into the conservative family — government accountability, transparency, and respect for taxpayers — had all either disappeared from the government of the day's playbook, or had been so severely compromised, sacrificed at the altar of electoral expediency, as to become unrecognizable. The government seemed to me to have become less and less accountable, less and less answerable to the elected Parliament.

At the same time as media attention was aroused by my departure from the Conservative caucus, a major political scandal was also being seized on by the press. The Harper government was embroiled in several controversies, the most notable one involving the Senate. Three senators appointed by the prime minister (and one other) were all under investigation for filing ineligible, possibly fraudulent, expense claims. More scandalous in my view, the executive (in the form of the chief of staff of the prime minister) "gifted" $90,000 to a sitting legislator in an alleged effort to make the scandal go away and salvage the reputation of the Conservative appointment and its key fundraising asset.

This action, representing an obvious lack of separation between the executive and legislative branches of the Canadian government, shocked many Canadians, and facilitated a RCMP investigation into both of those branches. What Canadians do not realize is that in the "Ottawa Bubble," that lack of separation is the norm — the executive constantly meddles in the affairs of the elected legislature, MPs, and even parliamentary committees.

Over the last generation, the executive has grown much too dominant and Parliament much too weak; in fact, things have become so bad that Parliament, supposedly the supreme legislative body in the land, could be described as subservient. Sadly, this has evolved to the point that the executive (the government) regards the legislative branch (Parliament) without respect, something that is merely an inconvenience. The executive has used prorogations to avoid a confidence vote and to shut down a parliamentary committee investigation regarding the possible transfer by Canadian soldiers of Afghan detainees to prisons where the danger of torture existed. These actions, in addition to its use of nearly seventy time-allocation motions in a single parliamentary session, provide convincing evidence of a government that would prefer to govern by fiat, Order-in-Council, and executive order, than be accountable and answerable to the elected Parliament.

❖

The result of an executive becoming increasingly unanswerable to Parliament, and therefore unaccountable, is that Canadian taxpayers and citizens are increasingly shut out of the decision-making process. If government listens only to its political advisors and its bureaucrats, paying only lip service to the notion that it is responsible to its citizens and its elected representatives, is it any wonder that it has grown in size and expense? Should we be surprised that government, in its modern, nanny-state form, controls not only more of our resources, but also more of our individual decision-making and liberties? Is it surprising that, as the cost of government increases, tax burdens similarly increase and, therefore, a taxpayer's disposable income, as a percentage, continues to decline? Is anybody shocked that governments at all levels are living beyond their means, or that the federal government alone is over $600 billion in debt?

Reinforcing the accountability of government to elected legislatures and councils (and, thus, citizens) is the only solution to this problem. If taxpayers do not demand greater accountability from governments of all stripes and levels for how those governments spend taxpayer resources, they cannot be surprised when governments and civil servants treat those resources like Monopoly money.

It is up to citizens, and their elected assemblies, to reassert control over the executive's treatment of public resources, because the executive has no incentive to do so on its own. It is time to recalibrate the relationship and the power structure between the executive and legislative branches of government. It is critical that we rebalance the influence wielded by the unelected executive and the elected Parliament, which at least in theory remains supreme.

The following analysis of how to correct this imbalance commences with an examination of how we got to where we are today. It all started in a tavern on Yonge Street in Toronto in 1837.

1.

THE QUEST FOR RESPONSIBLE GOVERNMENT: FROM THE MAGNA CARTA TO LORD DURHAM

I enjoy speaking to students about my job as a Member of Parliament. Most elementary and junior high school students have little idea what an MP is or does. They do, however, understand what a rule is and are accustomed to rules both at school and at home. When I explain that Parliament makes law and that laws are essentially rules that apply to everyone, the students gain at least some frame of reference.

In contrast, some high-school students are quite politically literate, some even politically active. When I ask them to define "responsible government" however, I am almost always disappointed with the response. Generally, without exception, "responsible government" will be defined as a government that governs responsibly, that is to say, one that makes good decisions.

The obvious problem with the answer is that determining what constitutes good governmental decisions requires a very subjective analysis. A social program, requiring a huge budgetary commitment, would quite likely be met with approval by a socialist. A fiscal conservative, however, might regard the proposal as unnecessary or even wasteful.

There is no objective method to determine what is a "responsible" decision or government initiative. However, in the context of our inherited Westminster system of government, "responsible government" has a very different and specific meaning.

The origins of parliamentary democracy and the quest for responsible government date back eight hundred years. In medieval Europe, a series of bodies developed to act as advisory bodies to the various monarchs. This was partly at the request of the monarchs, who saw value in counsel for affairs of court, and partly in response to the requests of the barons, commoners, and the church, who were all coming of age and believed that they were entitled to a say in governance.

The actual use of the word *parliament* traces its origins to 1236 and King John of England.[1] King John had, since his coronation, surrounded himself with advisors, trusted men appointed by him to help him make decisions on important matters. This group was called the *King's Council*. This tradition has been continued to this day, as the legal community bestows upon worthy members of its profession the designation *Queen's Counsel*.

However, the nobles and wealthy men of the time wished to have more say and they put pressure on King John to formalize a sharing of power. Following a period of conflict, John agreed to the principle of common consent, and the rules governing this sharing of power were set down in what is known as the *Magna Carta*, or Great Charter. As a result, King John had to expand his inner circle to include not only more nobles, i.e., the aristocracy and the landed gentry, but also more commoners. Thereafter, the precedent was established that the king would submit all requests for increased taxation to a newly created body of commoners, i.e., rich merchants and lawyers. Over several centuries the two distinct groups would evolve into the House of Lords and the House of Commons respectively.

This was the genesis of parliamentary governance, crude but appropriate for its time. We inherited this evolving system, at least in principle, on February 10, 1763, when France ceded its North American empire (New France) to Great Britain pursuant to the Treaty of Paris following the Seven Years' War. The "Royal Proclamation" of the same year established the legal parameters of the new British North America. The British North American colonies were distinct and were known by recognizable names such as Quebec, New Brunswick, Nova Scotia, and the islands of Prince Edward and Newfoundland. The mechanism of the "Constitutional Act" (properly known as the Clergy Endowments (Canada) Act) of 1791, divided Quebec into two separate colonies, English Upper Canada and French Lower Canada, with the Ottawa River serving as the border between the two. The terms *Upper* and *Lower* refer to the flow of the St. Lawrence River (eastward from the Great Lakes).

In the post–American Revolution period, Great Britain was suspect of too much democracy, which it feared might lead to "mob rule" in its remaining colonies. Accordingly, it deliberately attempted to counter rampant republicanism by strengthening the power and prestige of the governor, the handpicked emissary put in charge of the colony. Colonial decisions would be entrusted to the governor and his unelected executive council (Council of Advisors).

The 1791 Constitutional Act clearly set up the power structure for the colonies of British North America. In charge was the governor, who represented the British Foreign Office. The executive council was appointed by the governor to help him manage and administer the colony. The elected legislative assembly was comprised entirely of male landowners and had no legislative authority; its function could be considered consultative at best.

This attempt at colonial governance created a rather dysfunctional situation. Admittedly, any attempt at running a distant colony would prove challenging. However, having an appointed council oversee an elected assembly was especially awkward. This poor soil somehow nourished the seeds of responsible government; but cultivating those seeds would be difficult process, and would require the extraordinary efforts of reform-minded revolutionaries.

Following the War of 1812, two such reformers emerged: in Lower Canada, the aristocrat Louis-Joseph Papineau; and, in Upper Canada, my personal hero, journalist William Lyon Mackenzie.[2]

The Constitutional Act of 1791 placed the elected assembly under control of the appointed council. Whenever the assembly refused to act as the governor or council desired, the usual "solution" was to dissolve the assembly, call for an election, and hope for a more co-operative assembly. These acts of refusal were the only actions available to the elected assemblies of both Upper and Lower Canada, for they could wield only negative power; they could block the council's initiatives, but they could not direct them. Because of a tradition that dated back to when King John agreed to submit his budget to Parliament, the governor's spending plans had to be approved by both the council and the elected assembly. As the assembly could not introduce a budget bill, the assembly's power was accordingly limited to blocking the executive's spending plans. The result was frequent gridlock.

This gridlock was made worse by the fact that near-oligarchies had evolved in all of the colonies, a situation that was especially true in Upper and Lower Canada — the Château Clique in Lower Canada, and in Upper Canada, the Family Compact. It was there that the majority of the European immigrants were settling. The established landowners did not want to share power and were suspicious of extending democracy, since they felt that it would prove a threat to their financial interests.

In Lower Canada, the wealthy merchant families, such as the Montreal-based McGills and Molsons, dominated the ruling Chateau Clique. Opposed to their position of privilege and status was the Parti Patriote, dominated by young, educated men who had been excluded from the council. The Parti Patriote gained control of the elected assembly and drew up the famous "Ninety-Two Resolutions," outlining their grievances against the governor's appointed council. In 1834, the elected assembly demanded that it be given control over public finances, and, in a move before its time, further demanded that the executive council be made responsible to the citizens by requiring that the governor select his council from the elected members of the assembly.

It took a distant and largely uninterested London little time to reject each of the Ninety-Two Resolutions. In response, Patriote leaders staged rallies to protest the British rejection of their demands. One of the main leaders was Louis-Joseph Papineau. An enigmatic mix of revolutionary and land-owning aristocrat, he was a passionate orator and he worked disappointed dissidents into frenzy. Papineau preferred oratory to violence, but other Patriote leaders believed that words were not enough to bring about change. When a British army unit was dispatched to disperse a mob protest that had assembled at St. Denis in the Richelieu Valley, it wandered into crossfire, and six of its soldiers were killed. Perhaps because he feared how the event, which became known as the Battle of St. Denis, might turn out, Papineau was not present.

Two days later, re-organized British soldiers attacked nearby St. Charles, killing sixty Patriotes and arresting most of its surviving leadership. Then, at St. Eustache, 1,400 British redcoats attacked and nearly another one hundred Patriotes were sacrificed.

Later, a second, equally unsuccessful attempt to overthrow the British was organized by Patriote leaders who had fled to the United States to avoid capture. The Lower Canada Rebellion had been quelled with little to show for the twenty-seven soldiers and nearly three hundred French Canadians who perished.

❖

An equally unsuccessful, much less violent, but significant rebellion was organized by the newspaper man William Lyon Mackenzie in Upper Canada. The social unrest was directed against the Family Compact, an oligarchy comprised of Tory-Anglican insiders. Mackenzie was especially outraged that three million acres of prime Upper Canada real estate had been dedicated as clergy reserves for the benefit of the Anglican Church.

Mackenzie was elected to the assembly by the citizens of York. Despised by the establishment, he was expelled from the assembly by the governor four times. Each time he was returned by his appreciative constituents.

Stalemate between the lieutenant-governor of Upper Canada and Mackenzie-led Reformers in the assembly was frequent. This led to problems in the governing of the colony, especially with regard to the raising of taxes. In 1836, events came to a head. Without funds to continue operating the government, Governor Bond Head dissolved the assembly and called for a fresh election. But he then crossed the line by campaigning for the Conservatives using his vast resources, including land, to gain electoral support. In the election that year, the Reformers were decimated.

Undeterred, Mackenzie used his newspaper to spread the cause of reform against the oligarchic Family Compact. He proposed a rebellion where the Compact would be overthrown and a democratic republic established in its place. Mackenzie organized six hundred men, who met at Montgomery's Tavern on Yonge Street in York. Armed with only pitchforks, muskets, and clubs, the would-be revolutionaries were deterred and dispersed by a single shot fired by the Toronto sheriff. Later, Governor Bond Head led a group of volunteers up Yonge Street and torched Montgomery's Tavern.

The Upper Canada Rebellion had been repelled without a single casualty. Subsequent attempts by Mackenzie to organize American-backed border raids from a base near Buffalo in New York State were equally unsuccessful, and its participants when captured were either hanged, imprisoned, or exiled to Australia.

❖

The rebellions in Upper and Lower Canada, although completely without success, set in motion a series of events that would lead to the establishment of responsible government, not only in the Canadian colonies but throughout all of the British Empire.

The British Colonial Office was clearly embarrassed by the rebellions. London did not like to have its authority challenged. Accordingly, the Earl of Durham, a reformer in his own right and champion of Britain's Reform Act of 1832, was dispatched to British North America and charged to report back on how to keep peace in the colonies. His report, titled the "Report on the Affairs of British North America," but colloquially referred to as the "Durham Report," would lead firstly to responsible government in the colonies and then self-government and Confederation a quarter century later.

Although the latter is more significant to most aspects of Canadian history, it is actually the establishment of responsible government that is more critical to an examination of how Canadians currently govern themselves and the current state of Canadian parliamentary democracy.

The 1838, "Durham Report" had three principle recommendations:

- that Upper and Lower Canada be united into a single province or colony, with one government administration and assembly;
- that the governor be required to choose his advisors (council) from amongst the elected members of the assembly; and
- that the colonies be granted jurisdiction over local and internal affairs. Henceforth the governor would only be responsible for colonial matters.

Durham was recommending that those living in the colonies be given the same parliamentary rights that had been enjoyed for centuries by citizens of Britain. The Foreign Office initially rejected Lord Durham's call for responsible government in the not-yet-mature colonies, but it did pass the 1840 Act of Union, uniting Upper and Lower Canada under a single administration and assembly.

A united Canada brought moderate reformers from Canada West and Canada East (the names for the two parts of the colony — what were, formerly, Upper Canada and Lower Canada) together to fight for a common cause. Moderate reformers Louis-Hippolyte LaFontaine and Robert Baldwin became instant friends, and worked together advocating a common cause. In the 1848 election, the Reformers overwhelmingly took control of the assembly. On March 10, 1848, a new progressive governor, Lord Elgin, asked LaFontaine to lead the government.

The next year, the assembly passed the contentious Rebellion Losses Bill, indemnifying Patriotes, who had lost property in the 1837 Rebellion in Lower Canada. English-speaking Tories in Montreal were outraged; they lobbied Lord Elgin that the traitors not be compensated, and they demanded that he not sign the bill.

However, Elgin, a progressive, signed the bill. According to him, it was an internal matter duly considered by an assembly that had been elected to make such decisions. Although Anglo-Tories rioted in Montreal, Lord Elgin gave royal assent to the Rebellion Losses Bill on April 25, 1849. Responsible government had been won in the united Canadas!

It should be noted that some months earlier, prospering Nova Scotia had already received responsible government, having done so without any of the drama or violence that preceded its arrival in the United Canada. In 1847, the reformers there, led by Joseph Howe, won a majority in the Nova Scotia assembly. In February 1848, they were asked to take control of the administration, forming the first responsible government in British North America and in the entire British Empire.

Although responsible government was, in part, a product of waning interest in mercantilism in London, the achievement cannot be overvalued.* By 1855, all of Britain's North American colonies had won responsible government (Newfoundland was the last). Henceforth, all of the colonies would be governed only according to the desires of their own inhabitants.

❖

So, why is this protracted history lesson important or relevant to an examination of the current state of democracy in Canada? It is the hard-fought-for principle of responsible government that guarantees that it is the elected assemblies that control the executive branch of government and not the other way around. Responsible government is the constitutionally enshrined convention that governments are responsible and accountable to the democratically elected assemblies. Responsible government ensures that if the elected assembly loses confidence in the government, or if the government loses the support of the assembly, the government can govern no more.

Under the British parliamentary system, we do not elect our governments, we elect our legislatures. This is a fundamental and frequently misunderstood concept. It is still the pre-

---

* Mercantalism was the main economic system used in the period from the sixteenth to eighteenth centuries. Its main goal was to increase a nation's wealth by imposing government regulation on all of the nation's commercial interests. It was believed that national strength could be maximized by limiting imports via tariffs and maximizing exports.

rogative of the governor general (or lieutenant-governor of a province) to ask an appropriate leader if he or she is able to form a government. By both convention and practical reality, the individual chosen will be the leader of the party in the assembly who has the confidence and support of the majority of the members of the assembly.[3]

When one party has a majority of seats in the assembly, the choice becomes obvious. However, when no party has a clear majority of seats in the assembly, that matter becomes more complicated. The queen's representative's first and most important constitutional function is to ensure that at all times Her Majesty has a government in place. In a situation where no party has a clear majority of members in the assembly, the person chosen will be the individual who has the support of the majority of assembly members, not necessarily the leader of the party with the most members.

Technically speaking, the person chosen to serve need not even be a member of the assembly, provided that he or she has the support and confidence of the majority of the members.

Twice, Christy Clark has been asked to form a government in British Columbia notwithstanding the fact that she was not a member of the legislative assembly at the time. In 2011, she became the leader of the B.C. Liberal Party but was not an MLA. She formed a government, chose a cabinet, and governed from the gallery of the Victoria assembly for several months before obtaining a seat in a by-election. Then, in the 2013 B.C. general election, her Liberals retained a majority of the seats, but she lost her own. She was still the premier and she chose a new cabinet. Within months she was able to win a seat, again in a by-election.

The point is that one can lead a government as long as, but only as long as, one has the support of the Legislature or Parliament, as the case may be.

Media often refer to governments as serving terms; technically this is incorrect. Although legislative assemblies and legislators serve terms, governments are elected without term. Governing is a continuous process, as there must at all times be a government in place. Accordingly, once sworn in, a first minister (prime minister or premier) remains so until he or she resigns from office and is replaced by a new leader who has the support and confidence of the assembly.

My political science professor at the University of Saskatchewan, David Smith, explained responsible government in a simple but profound way: those who advise the Crown must command the support of the popularly elected chamber. Lose the confidence of the House and you must resign.

Canadian voters elect legislators; they do not select governments — that is the responsibility of the queen's representative. Accordingly, if democracy is to be maintained, the legislative branch must remain supreme and the government accountable and responsible to it.

When the government of the day ceases to be responsible to Parliament, responsible government is lost and democracy is imperilled. As we shall explore in the following chapters, that is exactly what is occurring in Canada today, and the product of this lack of accountability is questionable decisions made by governments that are not responsible in either meaning of the term.

2.

PUBLIC DEBT: A RUNAWAY TRAIN WRECK

Canada is in debt. In 2014, the federal public debt is in excess of $600 billion; if you are Canadian, your share of that federal accumulated debt is $17,500. The debt grows by over $49 million every day; over $2 million every hour.[1]

These numbers are staggering, but they tell only a partial story. The provinces and territories have amassed in excess of half a trillion dollars in debt as well: $547 billion to be exact.[2] Accordingly, Canada's total public debt is a just shy of $1.2 trillion, or a sobering $33,800 per Canadian (exclusive of unfunded pension liabilities).

Currently, eleven cents of every tax dollar goes toward servicing the above debt.[3] If Canada could have avoided paying $31 billion in interest, it would have recorded surpluses in the last several fiscal years. No past debt would have meant no current deficit!

The International Monetary Fund has warned that if Canada does not reduce its spending from 43 percent to 38 percent of its gross domestic product (GDP), the inevitable result will be higher tax burdens, dangerous debt loads, or both.[4] As countries of Western Europe such as Greece, Italy, Portugal, and even Great Britain have all painfully demonstrated, growth in public sector spending in excess in the growth of the economy cannot continue indefinitely. High deficits and growing public debt inevitably lead to higher interest rates, higher exchange rates because of a devalued currency, and eventually to capital leaving the country.

There are other direct and immediate consequences of public borrowing. With eleven cents of every tax dollar going to pay interest on the federal debt, that is 11 percent of federal revenues available to fund programs and services. The current generation must pay for past borrowing and therefore deny itself 11 percent of the services it is actually paying for. The same will be true tomorrow. Public debt mortgages our country's future and imposes higher taxes on future generations, who will be forced to pay for our current borrowing. Paying taxes for a previous generation's consumption is the ultimate violation of the principle of "no taxation without representation!"

But the principle of no taxation without representation exists to ensure that taxpayers are not overly burdened. Parliament was created in the thirteenth century when King John agreed to submit his requests for taxes to a House of Commons. This time-honoured principle remains, at least in theory, to the present day. The government must submit its spending estimates to the democratically elected Parliament. The government can only spend money once Parliament has approved and authorized it.

But in the last half-century, Parliament's ability to hold government to account has declined significantly. At the same time, Parliament's ability to control the public purse strings has been increasingly compromised, and now is almost completely neutered. The result of this increasingly weakened parliamentary oversight of federal public spending has been a runaway train of spending and dangerously accelerating public debt.

In 1970, the federal public debt was $15.3 billion. By 1980, it had grown to $61.6 billion. By 1990, it had exploded to $336 billion. In 2000, it had grown at a somewhat decelerated rate to $550 billion. It actually fell to $477 billion by 2010; but recent out-of-control spending has caused the federal public debt to grow to $526 billion in 2011, $558 billion in 2012, $587 billion in 2013, and $616 billion by the beginning of 2014.[5]

From $15 billion to over $600 billion in forty-three years, with over $125 billion of that additional debt added under the watch of the current Conservative government.

According to the Fraser Institute, "The bottom line is that the Conservative government is simply not budgeting in a conservative manner. Not only is it failing to conservatively forecast GDP growth and revenues, or [put] … forth realistic spending projections, it is not dealing with the root cause of the deficit: excessive increases in spending."[6]

With the entire Canadian public debt, including that of the provinces, in excess of $1.2 trillion, many economists have warned all Canadian governments to stop searching for additional revenue sources and spend more time and energy finding ways to curtail and reduce their own profligate spending habits.

Several interrelated occurrences allowed Canada to increase its public debt by a factor of four hundred in less than fifty years. The first was Canadian society's transformation from a post–Second World War industrial state to a welfare state and eventually to an entitlement state. Changing and increasing public demands encouraged governments' attempts to do more and more. Social-engineering bureaucrats were only too eager to design programs to improve the human condition and to attempt to satisfy a growing population's insatiable demand for programs and services that somebody other than they would pay for.

The second factor, occurring at almost exactly the same time, was a slow destruction of government's tools for ensuring financial accountability. Sequentially, our system of public financial checks and balances was eroding. The second trend allowed the first trend to progress unabated. Government could spend money, confident that there existed inadequate (and, eventually, virtually non-existent) effective oversight. Parliament's eight-hundred-year-old role in authorizing expenditures of the Crown and controlling the public purse strings was effectively coming to an end.

The consequence would be a federal state, with combined federal, provincial, and territorial debt of $1.2 trillion.

1. THE ENTITLEMENT STATE

In the last half-century, Canada has transformed itself from a welfare state to an entitlement state. Mark Milke of the Fraser Institute defines an entitlement state as one "where everyone feels they are entitled to a handout or a guaranteed income or a perfect life courtesy of other people."[7]

In 1962, in my home province of Saskatchewan, doctors went on strike and picketed outside of the Saskatchewan Legislature to protest against socialized medicare. A half-century later, almost any cut to any social program or even perceived inadequacy in the provision of that program (such as protracted surgical wait times) would result in public outcry and probable protest by the group or special interest affected. Our collective attitudes toward the role of the state in our lives have certainly seen gargantuan shifts during my lifetime.

Those changes continue today. The welfare state policies of the 1960s and 1970s, such as medicare, old age security (OAS), and Unemployment Insurance (now called Employment Insurance) have been joined by more-recent entitlement programs. Welfare-state programs were designed to provide necessary services and programs to those who were truly disadvantaged or were imperilled through no fault of their own. Entitlement programs, however, seek to improve the human condition irrespective of the group lobbying for the project's situation, financial or otherwise. Museums, art galleries, opera houses, and arenas to house professional hockey teams, cater disproportionately to the most, not the least, fortunate members of society.

Moreover, there appears to be a real disconnect between government and the taxpayers it is pretending to represent. Fiscal conservatives understand intuitively that government does not create wealth and has no money or resources except for that which it taxes from its citizens and corporations. Fiscal spendthrifts believe, erroneously, that government can magically create resources of its own, and therefore can spend its fairy dust generously on all projects and programs without consequence. Most Canadians would likely fall into this latter category. But government has no fairy dust and does not create wealth; it merely redistributes wealth. It spends only resources taxed out of the private economy. When a government offers to a build an electorally popular project, it is bribing the electorate with its own money. As Margaret Thatcher famously said, "there's no such thing as an entitlement, unless someone has first met an obligation."[8]

This reality would be sustainable if government spending grew only in proportion to the growth in the economy. Both income and corporate taxes increase as GDP increases, and if government spending grew in sync with economic growth, there would be no public debt. But it is when the former grows unchecked, without sufficient regard for growth in the latter, that we find ourselves with over $600 billion of federal government debt.

The predominant economic theory of the 1960s and 1970s was that of John Maynard Keynes. According to Keynesian theory, society can borrow its way into prosperity. More precisely, during times of recession or minimal economic growth, governments can stimulate demand by borrowing, thereby creating economic growth. That may or may not be true economically; regardless, it is imperative that if borrowing occurs during recessed times that the monies be repaid during prosperous times.

However, reckless politicians, supported by special-interest groups, began attempting too much, and once a program was provided, it became politically difficult, if not impossible, to take it away. Moreover, convinced that the good economic times were here to stay, the same reckless decision-makers reneged on the obligation to repay debt when the economy was strong, preferring to delude themselves into believing that good economic times meant they could spend even more recklessly, frequently doing so "like drunken sailors."

The provinces, municipalities, public-sector unions, and eventually even private business lobbied government to share the wealth during good times and stimulate demand in bad.

The result of bad political choices, based on a misunderstanding of economics, was decades of expensive and inefficient multi-level funding arrangements; a growing public sector, with pay, benefits, and pensions in excess of the private sector workers paying them; and, most troubling, industrial subsidies and corporate bailouts that took taxes from functioning parts of the economy to subsidize non-functioning sectors.

Industrial subsidies and corporate bailouts are perhaps the most troubling contributor to public debt. The public interest in supporting private enterprise is dubious, and there is growing economic data to show that subsidies and corporate welfare create neither economic growth nor stimulate jobs.[9] As the dollars used were originally taxed from sectors of the economy not requiring subsidy, the effect of industrial subsidy is to remove wealth from the functioning economy to prop up the parts working not quite so well.

Regardless, Industry Canada has disbursed $22.1 billion over the last half-century.[10] Again, $22.1 billion have been transferred from wealth-creating portions of the economy to support private, for-profit businesses apparently requiring subsidy to survive and/or grow. Of that money, $8.8 billion was dispersed in grants without even the prospect or expectation of repayment. Some dubious recipients of industrial subsidy, besides the giant car manufactures, include a bakery in Edmonton — it was given $1 million to develop gluten-free product lines of bakery items; other recipients include hot dog vendors, ice cream shops, pizzerias, and gas bars. A perusal of the list confirms numerous recipients received more than one grant, indicating that these subsidies become virtually permanent and the recipients dependent upon them. Why run your business more efficiently if Industry Canada has a program to subsidize your inefficiency?

Keynes understood that during times of recession, government spending could stimulate the economy; however, he never fully contemplated that future generations would endure reduced demand and investment due to its obligations to pay for the consumption of the previous generation. Paying back debt usually necessitates difficult and unpleasant actions, none of which are likely to improve the popularity of a government, so it is little wonder that governments rarely stop borrowing and even more infrequently pay back debt.

In 1970, all Canadian public spending (federal, provincial, and municipal) equalled 35 percent of GDP. By 1992 it had ballooned to 52 percent, but has been reduced to 41 percent currently.[11] However, the debt is growing again and is on track to do so for the foreseeable future. As a result, future generations will be forced to pay not only for the programs and services they consume; they will also be required to pay an excess of taxes to cover the debt of previous generations.

2. THE DEATH OF FISCAL ACCOUNTABILITY

The public may feel a sense of entitlement and have an insatiable demand for government programs and services. Social-engineering bureaucrats and vote-seeking politicians might want to satisfy every craving and spend, spend, spend. But Parliament controls the purse strings. Parliament must authorize spending for the government to legally spend.

Surely Parliament, as guardian of the public purse strings, will ensure that government spending is appropriate and that taxpayers receive value for money.

However, tragically, Parliament's oversight of public finances is almost non-existent. Concurrent to the demise of responsible government generally, Parliament has surrendered its traditional and constitutional role of providing financial oversight. With few exceptions, an emasculated Parliament provides almost no fiscal oversight; the Government of Canada spends as the Government of Canada wants to spend.

❖

Canadians do not directly elect their governments; we elect our legislatures. If the government is not accountable to the elected Parliament, that government, by definition, is unaccountable.

For close to a hundred years, Canadian governments generally ran balanced budgets; successive finance ministers viewed the public finances as money held in trust for the Canadian people. They only spent what was necessary and balancing the budget was the norm. If a deficit was absolutely necessary, such as during the two world wars, the money was repaid in a timely manner once the exigency concluded.

Meanwhile, Parliament scrutinized all spending, department by department and line by line. As the size of government grew, though, this became an increasingly complex and time-consuming exercise. Accordingly, shortcuts were pursued to make parliamentary scrutiny more "efficient." By the late 1960s, the system would come unwound; Parliament would surrender its most important role — guardian of the public purse strings.

In theory, and at one time in practice, Parliament would get to see the government's spending plans as they were being tabled, in order to scrutinize said plans. The process by which departments estimate their spending plans for the coming fiscal year is appropriately called the "tabling of the estimates." In minute detail, the estimates listed the department's estimated or requested spending plans; each program is listed and estimated line by line. Only after Parliament had approved the estimates could the department legally spend the monies.

However, as government grew in the 1960s, the estimates became more voluminous, and Members of Parliament would get lost in a maze of lines and numbers. Scrutinizing of these detailed spending estimates would go into the dog days of summer, when MPs were thinking about the barbecue circuit and looking for an exit from Ottawa's humidity. In the end, approving the estimates was growing too complex and time-consuming; rather than try to tackle the problem, most MPs elected to simply glance over the documents, rubber-stamping them; the process becoming little more than a formality. Eventually, government mandarins were so convinced that the estimates would be approved that they would proceed on that assumption. So the system of oversight was "reformed to make it more efficient." In December of 1968, the House amended its standing orders. Reform resulted in the Standing Committees of the House being tasked with approving the estimates for the various departments, which fell under its jurisdiction. The committees would have to report the estimates back to the House by May 31 of each year, failing which they would be "deemed to have been reported." The full House of Commons would then have until June 30 to vote on the main estimates. No longer would MPs have to scrutinize government spending once the kids were out of school!

For agreeing to delegate detailed scrutiny of supply to the House's standing committees, the Opposition was granted twenty-five "supply days," during which it would be able to move motions.

The system was breaking down, but it was not until 1972 that the demise of parliamentary oversight became complete. The end of the supply period was moved forward seven days to June 23, and Opposition supply days were reduced to twenty-two. If the estimates were not approved by the House by June 23, they would be deemed to be approved; Parliament had lost its most effective tool in holding government to account.

Under Standing Order 81(4)(a),[12] the leader of the Official Opposition may select the main estimates of two departments for consideration by the Committee of the Whole for a period not to exceed four hours. The rationale is that allowing a more selective focus on a couple of departments allows for a detailed examination.

During the Committee of the Whole, the Speaker vacates the chair and the minister of the chosen department brings officials and deputies onto the floor to assist in the answering of detailed questions. However, after the prescribed four hours has expired, the estimates are deemed approved and reported.

Moreover, whether examination of estimates occurs in the House committees or in front of the Committee of the Whole very little actual examination of numbers and spending plans occurs. Members, from all sides, prefer broad policy questions to any actual examination of the government's spending plans.

For the last forty plus years, the spending plans for the departments of the Government of Canada have essentially been given automatic approval. Moreover, changes in internal administrative processes have allowed for more line items to be lumped together in broad categories. Line-by-line approval in the committees has been replaced by approval of a "grouping" of items. It is easy to hide spending within a broad grouping of expenditure estimates. Amalgamation of substantive line items has meant that critical information has been merged and lost, as has been financial accountability.

However, Parliament is not the only institution of oversight that has had its ability to monitor the government's financial accountability diminished. The role of the Office of the Comptroller General was created to help rein in spending before it occurred. The mandate of the comptroller general was to assess spending approved by Parliament and ensure that there was actually enough money available to spend as Parliament had authorized. The Office of the Comptroller General was a check in the system and provided objective analysis as to whether, in fact, authorized spending was affordable and whether the government could cover its spending plans. This system was based on the understanding, commonplace in the days before serial deficit financing, that you cannot spend money that you do not have.

However, the office was neutered, based largely on the recommendations of the 1962 Glassco Report.[13] Glassco recommended removing bottlenecks of inefficiency in the system, thereby allowing managers to manage.

Of course, what Glassco considered bottlenecks I would have considered checks and balances. Regardless, the function of the comptroller general was transferred to the Treasury Board in 1967, and then eviscerated. In 1969, the office was abolished altogether. The comptroller general was re-established in 1978, but as a comptroller, it exists now only nominally and with a diminished role. The role of certifying and authorizing all department expenditures has been long removed and has been replaced by such functions as program evaluation, the provision of internal audits, supervision of procurement, real property management, and financial risk management.

What was once a powerful spending watchdog is now a mere staff agency within the Treasury Board Secretariat. The comptroller general provides financial management and functional direction, but in no way is it a check or balance over government finances themselves.

By the early 1970s, the government had effectively dismantled and/or assumed all the roles of budgetary oversight. Thereafter, government grew and overspent, resulting in growing deficits and, eventually, $600 plus billion in national debt. Government spends as it wants to spend and the people's elected Parliament merely stands by and watches.

❖

With all of the checks and balances of financial oversight effectively neutered, there has been no shortage of financial scandals, debacles, and boondoggles. It has fallen to the Office of the Auditor General and the newly created Office of the Parliamentary

Budget Officer to hold government to account for its annual expenditures in excess of a quarter trillion dollars.

But as we shall see below, the auditor general (AG) only audits money that has already been spent. Its work, although increasingly valuable, is akin to closing the barn door after the cattle have all bolted. The hope is that you will learn something by the audit that will retain the cows in the future. The role of the parliamentary budget officer (PBO) had been designed to monitor the cattle before and as they were leaving. However, as we shall see in a subsequent chapter on the Public Service, the government that created PBO subsequently deliberately attempted to control it. Then it moved to politicize it. Eventually, it has tried discredit it. This change in the government's relationship with the PBO has severely compromised the latter, ruining what could have been an effective and much needed check on government spending. The result has been a litany of deplorable spending decisions and mistakes.

In April of 2013, the auditor general reported that the federal government had lost track of $3.1 billion devoted to combating terrorism.[14] Between 2001 and 2009, the federal government allocated $12.9 billion across thirty-five departments and agencies with some aspect of public security in their mandate. But the AG reported that only $9.8 billion could be identified as having been properly spent. There was no allegation that the money was stolen or misappropriated, but 25 percent of the monies allocated could not be traced. Some was no doubt moved to other priority areas, while some was likely simply not spent since it was not allocated within the timeframe of the approved budget window.

The auditor general stated that the departments and agencies were required by law to report to the Treasury Board Secretariat on how the money was spent; but when the AG asked to see the reports, they were advised that they had not been prepared as required. Although most of the money was eventually traced, the fact that such a large amount of money could go missing shows what can happen when Parliament allows line items to be bundled together in the estimates: a breakdown in financial accountability.

Another recent example of the consequences of diminished financial oversight is the $2.5 million in advertising for the non-existent 2013 Canada Job Grant.[15] In this instance, the government continued to shill for this co-sponsored training program long after every province had refused to participate. Although no program existed, the government spent millions of dollars touting its supposed efforts in this area. Beyond that, government advertising generally is now in excess of $100 million annually. Much of it is ineffective, containing little valuable information; instead, it is often filled with little more than blatant partisan messaging.

A larger boondoggle was revealed on April 11, 2011, when it was reported that the federal government misinformed Parliament to win approval for a $50 million G8 fund that lavished money on dubious "security" projects in several Conservative ridings, including that of Treasury Board President Tony Clement. Auditor General Sheila Fraser reported that the process by which the fund was approved "may have been illegal."[16]

And of course there was the Sponsorship Scandal, when for six years money was transferred to Liberal-friendly advertising agencies without competitive bids and sometimes without any actual work being done. The auditor general called the practice "scandalous" and "appalling." Sheila Fraser concluded that $100 million was paid to a variety of Quebec communications agencies and that the program was designed to generate commissions for these agencies rather than produce any work of value for Canadians.

But the worst example of a lack of financial accountability occurred in 2000, when an internal audit at Human Resources discovered that $1 billion in employment program grants could not be traced.[17] There was no paper trail to determine if the money was properly spent or if the promised jobs were created.

As the above examples painfully illustrate, although audits are invaluable in reconstructing a scandal, boondoggle, or misappropriation, they obviously cannot prevent misspending. Regardless, the Office of the Auditor General is essential in determining if proper accounts are being kept, if money is spent for the purpose stipulated by Parliament, if effective spending controls are in place, and if generally accepted accounting principles are being followed.

The value of the auditor general's reports is in how the government reacts and improves financial reporting. But as an after-the-fact evaluator, the AG does not and cannot exercise control over real-time spending. Only Parliament can do this; unfortunately, as the case below demonstrates, its ability to do so has been emasculated.

Perhaps the lowest point in the devolution of responsible government and financial oversight in Canada occurred in the spring of 2011. For the first time in Canada, indeed, for the first time in the entire British Commonwealth, a government was about to be held in contempt of Parliament.

The sad story began the previous October; the Finance Committee had requested estimates for a number of big-ticket government projects. The cost of acquiring F-35 fighter jets, the forgone revenue of corporate tax cuts, the costs associated with hosting the G20 summit and various crime bills, were all on the committee's radar. The 40th Parliament was a minority Parliament; as a result, the Conservatives had five voting members on each committee, compared to three Liberals, two Bloc Québécois, and one NDP member, for a total of six combined opposition votes. Accordingly, the production motion passed; for four months, the government procrastinated, eventually only offering partial answers. The majority of the committee then found the government in contempt of Parliament for not complying with a motion of a standing committee of the House of Commons. Thereafter, then–Liberal Leader Michael Ignatieff used one of his supply days, mentioned earlier, to move a motion of non-confidence in the government.

A vote of non-confidence, according to the Leader of the Official Opposition, would confirm our commitment to parliamentary democracy and its fundamental principles. The chief principle that had been compromised was the government's obligation to "provide Members of the House with the information they need in order to hold the government accountable to the people of Canada." In an impressive speech defending responsible government, Ignatieff stated that "when Government fails in this most elementary task of democratic freedom, it is the duty of the Members of the House to bring the government down."[18]

The motion of non-confidence came to a vote in late March of 2011. The motion carried by a vote of 165 to 145, predictably breaking entirely on party lines. As a fiscal conservative, I am now embarrassed by my vote of "nay," but drunk on the daily diet of "partisan, coalition-conspiracy" Kool-Aid, I certainly did not feel ashamed at the time.

In kicking off his campaign, the Liberal leader claimed that the Canadian people will "have the opportunity to replace an arrogant government with one that respects democracy."

For being the leader of the first government, not only in Canadian history, but in the history of the entire British Commonwealth, to have been found in contempt of Parliament, the Canadian electorate "punished" the prime minister by electing 166 Conservative MPs, giving Stephen Harper his long-desired majority government. Responsible government was actually borne out: lose the confidence of the House and it is necessary to either resign or seek a fresh mandate from the electorate. But financial oversight was now a distant memory. A minority government could withhold relevant financial information, be found in contempt of Parliament, lose the confidence of the House, and then be returned with a majority!

With the check and balance of financial scrutiny diluted beyond repair, safeguards against irresponsible spending have been severely compromised. The emasculation of the comptroller general and the practice of deeming estimates approved on June 23, rather than actually vetting them, has resulted in the destruction of parliamentary oversight, overspending, and the death of financial accountability. The events leading to the election in the spring of 2011 confirmed that a government can ignore legitimate parliamentary requests with complete impunity.

In the forty-five years since Canada starting disassembling financial oversight, spending has increased in both good and bad economic times, resulting in growing deficits and accumulated debt. With an accumulated debt of over $600 billion dollars — a debt that is growing by $49 million every day — we will be paying for these bad decisions and this deficient financial oversight for generations.

3.

FEDERAL-PROVINCIAL COST SHARING: THERE IS ONLY ONE TAXPAYER

Long before I left the Conservative caucus, I had developed a reputation for fiscal hawkishness. I believe that taxpayers are entitled to expect that their governments, at all levels, spend their tax dollars prudently.

In times of fiscal restraint, this kind of prudence requires carefully prioritizing projects and ensuring that those funded are done so on a cost-efficient basis to ensure that taxpayers receive value for money. Spending only where necessary invariably requires an examination of responsibility for the proposed project. Is it something that could be better managed, or funded, by the private sector? Is it a matter that could be better undertaken by the non-profit, charitable, or philanthropic sectors? And, most critically, once a project is indeed deemed to be for the public good and therefore ought to involve public financing, what level(s) of government is the most appropriate to fund it?

Canada is a federal state, with, for the most part, a clear division of powers. The division of powers is set out in the Constitution Act in sections 91 and 92, where enumerated powers are listed for the various levels of government.

A non-exhaustive list of federal responsibilities include criminal law, national defence, national security, border security, coastal security, native persons and native lands, fisheries and oceans, old age security and pensions, unemployment insurance, and provincial equalization.

The legislative matters assigned to the provinces include hospitals and health care, education, provincial highways and social assistance. Municipalities receive their powers and authority directly from the provinces, and the matters they are responsible for are local in nature and include streets, curbs, sidewalks, gutters, parking, snow removal, pets, utilities, and public transit.

As a newly elected Conservative MP, one of my first very public criticisms of the Conservative government occurred in November 2011, when I voiced opposition to the federal government's decision to contribute $100 million toward the construction of the Royal Alberta Museum. Having an appreciation for history, education, and tourism, I was not opposed to the museum conceptually; however, with all three levels of government running growing deficits, I certainly questioned the project's affordability and was definitely opposed to the proposed funding model.

I believe that governments must distinguish between wants and needs; and must focus on the latter, providing basic, essential and required services to their population. "Wants" must be deferred until they become affordable. With the federal government running a nearly $50 billion deficit, I felt that 2011 was not that time.

Moreover, I could find no authority in section 91 of the Constitution Act that makes the federal government responsible for, or, for that matter, expressly authorizes, funding local or provincial museums. The federal government does build and operate many great museums and galleries. I suspect, however, that neither the Province of Alberta nor the City of Edmonton contributed to the National Art Gallery.

The sad reality, though, is that many Canadians generally, and proponents of these projects specifically, believe that if a proposed project is perceived to be meritorious, all levels of government should automatically fund it on that basis, without regard to which level of government in fact has jurisdiction and responsibility for project funding.

Remembering that there is only one taxpayer, the question becomes: what possible advantage is there to involving all three levels of government in funding a project? If one believes that government is by nature expensive and inefficient, it is a logical conclusion that involving multiple levels of government exponentially increases the prospects for waste and mismanagement. Whenever jurisdiction is assumed by more than one government, the inevitable result will be argument, confrontation, delay, and increased cost.

In fact, the differences that arose as a result of the varied engineering standards of the respective levels of governments threatened the signing of the Memorandum of Agreement for the building of the Royal Alberta Museum. In the end, the agreement was signed just before the expiration of the federal Building Canada Fund. Two plus years later, the ground was still not broken; but the "Economic Action Plan" signs had been erected! It was not until January 2014 that construction commenced on the Royal Alberta Museum in downtown Edmonton.

Respective levels of government also have different priorities. The Building Canada Fund and one of its predecessor programs, Canada Works, were designed specifically to help cash-strapped municipalities repair crumbling infrastructure in aging cities. However, politicians soon realized that sewers and potholes were less valuable politically then sexy, high-profile, artsy, and athletic megaprojects like the aforementioned Royal Alberta Museum.

Cutting the ribbon to a new sports arena or concert hall makes for a much better photo opportunity than opening a sewage treatment plant. As a result, replacing critical infrastructure (needs) gave way to the irresistible appeal of building more culturally and socially appealing megaprojects (wants). Ironically, municipal decision makers, who would have been in the best position to assess local needs, were frequently squeezed out of the final project selection process by the higher levels of government because of the latter's deeper pockets.

❖

The creep toward blurred constitutional lines of authority started almost a half-century ago. It was at that time that the concept of "delegation" was first introduced. According to that concept, one level of government could agree to delegate spending authority to another level.[1] In practical terms, this meant that the federal government was able to use its spending powers for programs in areas in which it does not have constitutional jurisdiction to legislate.

As the welfare state developed, the first such provincial areas "delegated" were heath, education, and welfare. In funding programs, conditional on the provincial delivery conforming to a certain standard, Ottawa was essentially circumventing the Constitution. By attaching conditions to the funding, the federal government was indirectly legislating in areas it formally could not, given its lack of constitutional jurisdiction.

Ottawa bureaucrats, interested in social engineering, were only too happy to design national programs requiring compliance with their national standards, even if the programs involved matters of exclusive provincial jurisdiction, such as health care and highways. Indeed, such programs eventually expanded to include municipal matters such as housing and crumbling municipal infrastructure.

Cash-strapped provincial and municipal politicians, mindful of the increased costs of a growing populations and the need to provide health care and education provincially and public transit and replace infrastructure in aging cities, were either happy to take the money or resigned to the notion that it was a necessity. In some cases, the federal government was even able to strong-arm the provinces to spend monies it may not otherwise have been inclined to, or risk losing the 50 percent federal contribution. The federal government introduced public medical health insurance and the Canada Assistance plan and offered to pick up 50 percent of the tab for the provinces that chose to participate.[2] However, whatever the case, the conditions prescribed were a constant irritant, always the subject of protracted negotiation, necessitating many bureaucrats. The delivery of the programs became equally complex, as the various departments from the various levels of government applied their differing procedures and processes for project management and evaluation.

The administrative cost of shared programs began to consume greater and greater portions of the funding envelopes.

Bureaucracies grew as multilevel institutional structures were improvised to administer these projects; programs and service delivery did not improve but costs soared. It is counterintuitive to believe that multiple bureaucratic structures, answering to different political masters, all with different priorities, would result in anything but inflated cost, inefficiency and delay.

There is only one taxpayer. Governments seem to be oblivious to the realty that regardless of which level of government is involved in financing a project, it is the same taxpayer who is contributing to that government's coffers. Having more than one level of government involved may produce what appears to be a sharing of the burden; however, given the exponentially increased cost of having multiple levels of bureaucracy administer the same project, the reality of attempted burden sharing is a significantly increased burden on the taxpayer bankrolling all levels of participating governments.

Surely it would be more cost effective to have one level of government design, approve, fund, build, monitor, and then maintain a public work. Having multiple bureaucracies in charge results in no one really being in charge, least of all the taxpayer, who is funding the tab for this bloated and inefficient delivery model. Such a solution would require a serious discussion regarding the rebalancing of constitutional authority so that taxing ability more closely aligns with jurisdictional responsibilities. But, the cumulative cost to the taxpayer would be significantly reduced if duplicate bureaucracies were eliminated and responsibility and accountability restored to a single level of government.

Cost-shared programs are currently so entrenched that they have essentially become institutionalized. Applicants believe that *any* mega project ought to be shared equally by the respective levels of government. The inefficiencies of having duplicated and triplicated bureaucracies administer the same programs aside, we have completely lost sight of the divisions of power in the Canadian Constitution.

In the process, accountability has been entirely compromised. When the lines of jurisdiction become blurred, the lines of accountability become complex and impossible to follow. When a cost-shared program or project goes sideways, who gets the blame? Which level of government will willingly take responsibility for a program or project that goes off the rails? It will eventually require an expensive audit, also at taxpayer expense, to finally resolve the issue!

1. FIND THE CAUSE
2. ASSIGN NO BLAME

Although the federal-provincial and three-way cost-sharing programs were designed to promote national standards and burden-sharing, their real effect has been to blur constitutional lines of responsibility and, as costs skyrocketed, end any concept of financial responsibility for the projects. The lines of responsibility have been irrevocably blurred and accountability for these projects compromised, if not destroyed. Taxpayers and citizens deserve a higher level of accountability and oversight from all levels of government for how their tax dollars are spent. The division of power was created to assure appropriate checks and balances within the federal state. Power must be divided, not concentrated, and always subject to review and preferably restraint.

4.

PARLIAMENT: A BROKEN INSTITUTION

Under the constitutional convention of responsible government, the government (the executive) is accountable and responsible to the Parliament of Canada. Yet the Canadian Parliament, including all of its constituent elements, is failing miserably in its constitutional obligation. My observations are institutional, not partisan nor personal. The problems are systemic and endemic; ironically, the only institution with the authority to remedy this glaring democratic deficit has no incentive to do so.

The current Conservative government treats Parliament as an inconvenience at best and with contempt at worst. The current executive routinely shuts down debate by implementing time allocation (it has imposed strict time limits on debate seventy times since the last election); it has prorogued Parliament to avoid a confidence motion it was sure it was going to lose, shut down a parliamentary committee investigating the transfer of Afghan detainees without obtaining assurances against torture, and to avoid, for over a month, answering awkward questions regarding the PMO involvement in the Senate Expenses Scandal. Finally, in 2011 the government was found in contempt of Parliament for its refusal to provide detailed cost estimates for hosting the G20 Summit and the cost of purchasing new fighter jets to the parliamentary committee studying the matter.

Amazingly, the government was not even embarrassed by being held in contempt of Parliament. In the election that followed Parliament's loss of confidence in the government, the Conservative Party of Canada (CPC) argued its detractors were playing partisan games and were conspiring to form a coalition government. As a result, the Conservative government was rewarded with a majority mandate by the electorate!

❖

The current government, somewhat reluctantly, acknowledges Parliament as a legislative body with lawmaking authority. But to the greatest extent possible, it prefers to run all aspects of Parliament rather than be accountable to it. The current government prefers to govern by Order-in-Council and executive edict as opposed to having to answer to an occasionally meddlesome Parliament.

As a result, the executive has so neutered the institutions of Parliament as to render them nearly impotent, practically unable to fulfill their constitutional duty to hold the executive to account. Any Ottawa insider will verify that almost nothing goes on in the Parliamentary Precinct without the Prime Minister's Office's knowledge, consent, and, increasingly frequently, direction.

Executive control and interference has converted all of the major components of the Parliament of Canada, changing them from serving as meaningful checks on government power to serving as placators, complicit in the government agenda The institutions of Parliament, which are failing Canadians in holding government to account, are the House of Commons, the committees of the House of Commons, the government caucus, and the Senate of Canada.

Constitutional expert Peter Russell once famously wrote that a Canadian prime minister with a majority mandate is like a U.S. president without a Congress.[1] Sadly, that is true; a prime minister who can control all of the Parliamentary Precinct can govern without being answerable to any of the constitutional checks and balances on prime ministerial authority. A prime minister in such an enviable power position will treat Parliament as a rubber stamp for his agenda, rather than a constitutional check on his government's power.

1. THE HOUSE OF COMMONS

Those who advise the Crown must command the support of the democratically elected chamber. The lower house, the House of Commons, is the democratically elected chamber and it is, in theory, the primary body in holding the government to account. In sad reality, the House of Commons serves as a rubber stamp for a majority government's agenda.

A House of Commons has existed since the thirteenth century when, following the signing of the Magna Carta, King John consented to submit his requests for increased taxes to an elected assembly. This elected legislature was designed specifically to represent the citizen taxpayers and provide a check against the Crown's insatiable appetite for more taxes. Eight hundred years later, these constitutional requirements still apply — the Crown (the executive) cannot spend money that Parliament has not approved. Money bills must be introduced in the elected House of Commons, not in the appointed Senate. No private MP can introduce a bill or initiative that requires the Crown to commit funds without the express approval of the government or a royal recommendation.

However, the House of Commons, especially one in a majority setting, has long abandoned assigning any value to its role of serving as a check on government spending or of vetting proposed government initiatives or legislation. There is a simple reason why this is the case: the members of the governing caucus think of themselves as part of the government, rather than a check on the government. They refer to the government using pronouns like "we" or as "our government." They go home on weekends armed with talking points and prewritten op-ed pieces to submit to local newspapers praising the government's performance and virtue. They show up at government-funding announcements in their ridings (or in nearby ridings if the riding is not served by a member of the governing caucus), often with oversized novelty cheques (sometimes bearing the party logo) bragging and taking credit for the pork that has just been delivered.

These MPs are of no value in holding the government to account; they consider themselves to be part of the government. They do not even pretend to be a check on the government. On a good day, they are cheerleaders for the government; on a bad day, they are government apologists. On all days, they are part of the communications machinery of government, as opposed to critical reviewers of government proposals. And nowhere is this dereliction of duty in providing a check on government more evident than in the daily proceedings of the House of Commons.

The majority of the House of Commons' day is spent debating government bills. The remainder is spent debating and voting on Opposition bills. One hour each day is reserved for debating private member bills or motions. However, most of the "debate" and all of the "votes" are so closely monitored, and, when necessary, orchestrated, by the Prime Minister's Office that any separation between the executive and the legislative branches is purely illusionary. Government backbenchers are encouraged to deliver speeches in favour of government legislation and in opposition to Opposition motions (unless of course the government supports the Opposition motion, in which case its backbenchers are expected to do likewise). Almost all members read from prepared text. The PMO prefers this method; freelancing might result in someone going off script. The department sponsoring the government bill, or potentially affected by an Opposition motion, will prepare speaking notes or complete canned speeches. Members of Parliament uncomfortable with the role of actor, reading the playwright's script, are encouraged to vet their own proposed comments with the designated government point person.

The entire process is a farce and resembles less of a debate than it does bad theatre. Not infrequently, a compliant parliamentarian will read a prepared text on a topic he or she is mostly unfamiliar with; that talk will be followed by a member from another party doing exactly the same thing, although staking out a different position. On several occasions, as a member of the Conservative caucus, I was handed a canned speech mere minutes before I was asked to present it, as the planned speaker had somehow been delayed. Literacy skills have replaced debating skills in what passes as a debate in the House of Commons.

It is almost unheard of for a member to address points raised by the previous speaker, which real debate would require. This is the obvious limitation of any "debate" advanced by prepared text, written by staffers, days before the "debate" has even commenced.

Eventually, the debate will collapse when there are no more speakers rising to participate or, more than likely, after the government has expedited the process by introducing a time allocation motion limiting further debate to a specified number of hours or days. Both the time allocation motion and then the vote on the merits of the bill or motion will be whipped. The party whips will produce voting instructions and actual instruction sheets will be distributed by parliamentary pages and placed on the desks of the elected MPs.

This is what parliamentary democracy has devolved into: elected MPs being issued voting instructions. So disengaged are many MPs that I have actually witnessed members confused as to what the current vote was and what the whipped party position was when multiple deferred votes are being taken. Too many times I have heard a disengaged member inquire of his or her neighbour: "Which vote are we on? We're voting 'yea,' right?"

I am ashamed to disclose that your elected MP is frequently so disengaged that he is not only reliant on his party whip for his voting instructions, but quite possibly will also need to be coached by mates only slightly more engaged in the process.

Elizabeth May, then the sole Member of Parliament representing the Green Party, tells the story of MPs of various party affiliations inquiring of her as to how she decides how she is going to vote on any particular bill or motion. She replies that she reads the bill, studies it, consults with her constituents, sometimes asks questions of the sponsor, and then comes to her position. Incredulous, MPs from other parties exclaim about how labour intensive that must be and how much easier it is to simply follow the voting instructions provided by the party whips! Undoubtedly that is true. However, I believe most constituents would be shocked to discover that their elected representatives are voting automatons, often too disengaged to even follow what item they are voting on.

I do not mean to be too critical of the whipped party voting machine. Given the complete lack of efficacy of the individual parliamentarian in having any input into, let alone impact on, a process completely dominated by government and party operatives, they cannot be overly blamed for losing interest and becoming disengaged.

Of course, there is nothing particularly new about whipped votes per se. Whipped votes on matters of confidence are as common, and have existed for as long as there have been parties in Parliament. However, as with all matters regarding the erosion of parliamentary democracy and responsible government, it is the increased use of whipped votes that should concern defenders of democracy.

The Reform Party, and its successor, the Canadian Alliance, had a party policy of free votes. The original constitution of the Conservative Party of Canada promoted free votes, except in matters of confidence, budget votes, and votes on the expenditure estimates. After the 2008 CPC convention in Winnipeg, the words "and core government initiatives" were somehow added to the list describing the exceptions to the free vote presumption, although no one that I have talked to can recall that matter ever being debated or voted on. Regardless, that addition has allowed the government whip to declare essentially all matters as core government priorities, and, as a result, every vote on every government bill or motion is now a whipped vote.

This now even applies to procedural motions such as time allocations. This change surprised me when I was a member of the CPC caucus, because I am unfamiliar with any party policy priority, much less any key one, that states the Conservative Party of Canada will place limits on debate on non-urgent matters and use its parliamentary majority to suppress the democratic process.

As difficult to accept as these changes are, it is the expansion of the whipped vote to include private member's business that even many loyal partisans find particularly odious.[2] For centuries, it was the prerogative of a Member of Parliament to forward a legislative bill or motion and have it adjudicated by his or her parliamentary peers without the meddling of the party leadership.

This is traditional and logical. By definition, a matter cannot be a core or key government or party priority if the government has chosen not to table a bill or motion on that particular subject. Accordingly, it ought to be open to private members to put forward a policy idea where the government has chosen not to.

There are many examples to demonstrate that the party leadership will not allow private MPs that privilege. On June 5, 2013, Conservative members of the Standing Committee on Access to Information, Privacy, and Ethics were whipped into eviscerating C-461, a private member's bill (which I sponsored) that would have allowed for specific salary disclosure for senior levels of the federal public service. The bill had widespread support in the CPC caucus until the government objected to allowing the public access to how much it is paying its senior people and disclosing how many civil servants were earning generous (six figure) performance bonuses.

When the government is able to whip its members to vote against a private member's bill, predominately supported by those members, the government's control over Parliament is complete. In the process, Parliament has surrendered its ability and role in holding government to account.

❖

The focal point of the House of Commons' day is between 2:15 and 3:00 p.m. Eastern Standard Time (11:15 a.m.–12:00 p.m. on Fridays). That is the holy grail of holding government to account: Question Period. QP is the forty-five minute period in the day when the House of Commons asks the executive to explain and defend its actions.

Although many commentators correctly observe that answers are provided only when the government wants to provide them, and that there are no rules against refusing to answer a question, making up your own question and then answering it, or uttering incoherent nonsense, eventually, with enough media attention, the government will pay a political price if it routinely attempts to evade important questions or to obfuscate when asked to defend its actions. For forty-five minutes, the Opposition is actually afforded a purposeful opportunity to live up to the expectations of holding government to account.

But holding government to account is Parliament's prerogative; it is not the exclusive role of the Opposition. Accordingly, backbench members of the governing party are afforded three questions per day. Recalling that the current government prefers its backbenchers to be an extension of its Communication Branch, rather than to ask actual questions that might have the potential to embarrass the government, it is little wonder that these questions are scripted, planted, and designed exclusively for the purpose of allowing the government to get some message out.

"Mr. Speaker, the government just yesterday completed a historical trade deal with Country X. Can the hard-working Minister of International Trade please advise the House as to what this deal will mean for Canadians in terms of jobs and economic growth?"

It is not so much a question as an infomercial.

Even more egregious, planted questions will frequently be used to attack a member of the Opposition. "Mr. Speaker: yesterday the Leader of Party Y mused about legalizing small amounts of marijuana (or criticized 'our' government's minimum mandatory sentences); can the Minister of Justice please tell this House why Party Y's soft-on-crime policies are bad for law-abiding Canadians?"

Such a question should be disallowed. Commenting on somebody else's statement or policy has nothing do with government business or policy; therefore, this type of "question" has no place in the forty-five important minutes allotted to the House to hold the government to account.

The use of government-planted questions from backbenchers is infantile, giving governments self-serving, leading opportunities, and allowing them even more avenues to practise their talking points. But worse, this practice denies the House of Commons three actual questions every day. That's fifteen opportunities per week to hold the government to account squandered, in favour of self-serving blather. However, if it were ever proposed that the governing party lose the right to ask puffball questions during Question Period, rest assured the government would aggressively defend the practice, hypocritically citing the important role of the backbench MP as a justification for planted question continuation.

❖

The fifteen minutes prior to Question Period are reserved for members' statements. A time-honoured tradition, Standing Order 31 allows private members, members who are not part of the executive council, to speak on any topic for up to sixty seconds. Traditionally, the period has been used for members to congratulate a local sports champion, honour a milestone birthday of a local volunteer, or eulogize a local philanthropist.

However, in the last few years, all parties have decided to politicize the members' statements (colloquially referred to as an SO 31). Generally, up to a third of these SO 31s will be used to attack an opposition member, or policy, or make a self-serving, free-standing political announcement. Countless CPC members' statements refer to the supposed NDP $21 billion Carbon Tax. The Opposition is no better, with the leadership encouraging its members to use their infrequent members' statements to chastise the government for its alleged complicity in the Senate Expenses Scandal.

Again, diverting members' statements away from their intended purpose is an attack on the few rights that private members maintain. Sadly, members anxious to gain favour with their party leadership are only too happy to participate in this political manipulation of Standing Order 31. But it is the government and opposition party leaders' vetting and approval of members' statements, prepared by the members themselves, that is truly compromising members' rights and establishing them as subservient to their leadership.

However, in the spring of 2013, there was a well-publicized and rare display of an MP standing up for himself. The MP for Langley raised a point of privilege, arguing that his rights as a Member of Parliament had been infringed upon in that he was denied his apportioned slot for an SO 31 member's statement because the "topic had not been approved." Without naming specifically who did not approve his member's statement, Mark Warawa correctly stated that it is only the Speaker who can reject an SO 31. Standing Order 31 states: "A Member may be recognized, under the provisions of Standing Order 30 (5), to make a statement of not more than one minute," and that "the Speaker may order a Member to resume his or her seat if in the Opinion of the Speaker improper use is made of this Standing Order."

The practice of members submitting their proposed members' statements to the House Leader's Office for vetting has developed lately, and, strangely, it has for the most part gone unchallenged, at least on the government side. Why private members would require the approval of the executive is a mystery, but it is further evidence of party leadership micromanaging MPs and converting them from watchdogs into cheerleaders.

According to the rules, only the Speaker can determine if the contents of a proposed SO 31 are inappropriate or if the statement exceeds the allotted one minute. The rules are there to protect the integrity of the House and the rights and responsibilities of its members. Neither private members' motions nor bills nor SO 31s are the prerogative of the whips or the House leaders; they are the prerogative of private members. The government controls so much of the parliamentary procedures and calendar, it is imperative that private members stand firm on defending the few rights and opportunities we maintain to raise matters of importance to our constituents.

Sadly, it is through blind ambition that MPs have, for the most part, allowed themselves to become puppets of their party leadership rather than using the rare opportunity to ask a question during Question Period or give an unvetted member's statement, holding the government to account and representing their constituents, respectively.

❖

The final topic to be canvassed regarding a change in Commons' procedure that has allowed the government to compromise the House's ability to force accountability is the government's increasing reliance on omnibus bills and, more recently, omnibus motions.

The House of Commons is supposed to vet, scrutinize, and, theoretically, improve government legislation. That becomes impossible when the government submits omnibus bills (lengthy bills containing changes to legislation in disparate areas). Time allocations, implicit in the standing orders or imposed by motion, provide inadequate time for MPs to scrutinize complex and lengthy pieces of legislation. The government understands this and submits such bills deliberately.

The most egregious recent example of an omnibus budget bill was the Budget Implementation Act of 2012,[3] which came in at over 1,100 pages. The bill had many non-budgetary items attached to it such as changes to the environmental assessment process.

Invariably, an omnibus budget bill will contain multiple wedge issues, which make it difficult for the opposition parties to vote against the legislation without also voting against a part of the bill that they otherwise would have supported. This kind of packaging allows the cabinet to gleefully point out in Question Period every time the opposition votes against a specific line item in the omnibus budget.

For example, if a question arises concerning the care and treatment of injured war veterans, the minister will take great delight in pointing out that the last budget bill contained a $x increase to the Department of Veterans Affairs, but the honourable member asking the question voted against it. Although that might be true, the MP only did so because he or she was wedged; he or she was not voting against the increase to the department or program under consideration but was voting "no" to the government's spending plans in their entirety.

In order to properly hold the government to account, it is necessary to break omnibus bills up into logical, bite-sized pieces. Doing so allows them to be properly vetted and then voted on individually rather than as part of an unmanageable package

More recently, we are beginning to see omnibus government motions also. In the first week back following prorogation in the fall of 2013, the government House leader introduced a single motion combining such completely unrelated concepts as: the reformation of parts of the MP expense regime, the restoration of the Special Parliamentary Committee on Missing and Murdered Aboriginal Women, and, notably, the restoration in its entirety the government's legislative agenda to the stage that it was at prior to the government's decision to prorogue. So, in order to vote for the continuation of a critical special committee engaged in an important study, the members were wedged into allowing the restoration of the government's legislative agenda, notwithstanding the longstanding rule that government bills die when the government opts for prorogation.

The government should not be allowed to package such unrelated concepts. In fact, in at least one instance the Speaker actually ruled in favour of an NDP request for partial severance. However, the growing reliance on long, disparate omnibus bills and motions is clearly a deliberate and calculated attempt by the government to prevent the House of Commons from holding it to account.

2. PARLIAMENTARY COMMITTEES

Committees of the House of Commons have traditionally played an important role in the vetting and improving of the legislation referred to them. Many committees of the House have worked together to improve and tweak legislation passed in principle by the entire House of Commons at Second Reading.

However, currently, the House committees have become so politicized that they have become completely useless at vetting or improving legislative initiatives. The committee process has been completely commandeered by the executive, most notably by the Prime Minister's Office.

Perhaps the clearest example of this is the above-referenced case of interference by the PMO and the minister of justice with the Access and Privacy Committee regarding PMB C-461, the private member's bill I introduced dealing with public sector salary disclosure. The government decided it was opposed to allowing the public access to such information and the PMO instructed compliant members of the committee to gut the bill.

The committee performed a charade in which they pretended to study the legislation. Not a single witness who testified was in favour of raising the salary disclosure bar. Regardless, amendments were proposed to raise the bar to a level that would ensure it would apply to no deputy minister, and then, without any debate on the amendment, compliant members of the committee did the PMO's bidding.

How is it possible that such a well-orchestrated political manoeuvre can be executed? It is the result of a little-known process not established by the standing orders, regarding committees: the pre-committee meeting. It is at the all-important pre-committee meeting that specific decisions are conveyed to the members of the caucus sitting on a specified committee. All concerns are addressed and the instructions are made clear by executive staffers to the elected committee members.

No detail is left to chance; the entire committee process is managed by executive staffers from the minister's office affected by the proceeding. When ministerial staff run into logistical problems that they have insufficient clout to resolve they call for back-up heavies from the PMO. Even the questioning of witnesses is decided on by executive staffers — they provide "suggested" questions for the use of the members when posing questions during committee hearings. If the minister is the witness, there is nothing "suggested" about the questions distributed to committee members — the distributed questions are scripts that are to be followed to the letter.

Similarly, decisions regarding amendments proposed by Opposition members are discussed, and a designated MP, generally the parliamentary secretary, will be provided with speaking notes as to why an opposition amendment is inappropriate and why the government members will not support it.

I used to pride myself on my ability to cross-examine hostile witnesses at Justice Committee meetings (that is, witnesses not supportive of the proposed government legislation). Although limited by strict time limits (often five minutes), I was nonetheless frequently able to poke holes in the witness's analysis or point out contradictions. However, I eventually learned that my contributions were not appreciated. As the hearings are a sham and voting instruction are determined by executive staffers prior to the commencement of the hearing, nobody really cares what evidence comes out or how it stands up to cross-examination. The entire process is a farcical show. Accordingly, the executive staffers would prefer it if members simply lobbed softball questions to supportive witness, rather than giving any more of the committee's limited time to unsupportive witnesses.

The entire committee process is micromanaged by executive staffers to the extent that the committee members are often little more than their puppets. As a result, there is no separation of powers between legislative committees and the executive.

❖

In April 2013, in an extraordinary meeting of the sub-committee of the Procedure and House Affairs Committee (PROC), which deals with the votability of private members' bills and motions, the sub-committee was considering Motion 408. M-408 would have condemned discrimination against females through sex-selective pregnancy termination. As is the procedure for vetting the votability of such bills and motions, the committee relies on the expert advice from an analyst regarding the constitutionality (both jurisdictional and Charter compliance)of an issue and whether the matter is redundant.

On these points, the analyst stated clearly his determination: "It is within federal jurisdiction. It does not offend the Constitution, and there's no similar motion currently on the Order Paper." In other words, the motion was, in the view of the non-partisan analyst, entirely votable.

After a couple of clarifying questions for the analyst, the Conservative member of the committee moved that "Bill C-408 should not be deemed vot[a]ble because it does not meet these two criteria." This motion was carried unanimously without any further discussion. So, with swift adjudication, Motion 408 was dead, prevented from being debated and voted on in the House of Commons.

What is disturbing about this, firstly, is the haste and carelessness with which the motion was dispatched. The mover of the motion three times referred to it as a bill, when, in actuality, M-408 was a motion. This is more than mere nitpicking; the analyst clearly pointed out in his analysis that the standard of review is different for bills than for motions. Because motions are not binding and do not invoke statutory rules, the test is relaxed slightly.[4] So, any misunderstanding of what the committee was considering was most relevant.

But what was more disturbing than the committee's haste was their apparent disregard for the rights of the private MP.

Private members may bring matters of importance up for debate in the form of motions or bills. In a parliamentary calendar largely comprised of government business, subject to rules and a lottery that determines precedence, this is the most significant tool a private member maintains.

Undoubtedly, the issue of pregnancy termination is a subject that makes some MPs uneasy and most party leaders nervous, but that is entirely irrelevant. If members are opposed to a motion, they can vote against it. If leaders are strongly opposed to it, they can use moral suasion, or, more likely, whip their caucuses to vote against a motion. But to essentially censor a motion right at the gate, against the advice of an independent analyst, is heavy-handed and, I would suggest, contrary to the expectations of constituents, who rightly believe that their MPs have a voice and can represent them in Ottawa.

Predictably, a subsequent appeal to the entire PROC Committee was conducted in camera (i.e., privately) and purportedly summarily dismissed. By moving the vote in camera, the government ensured that the public would not know what, if anything, the committee considered before dismissing the appeal. This is a disturbing trend: moving the operation of committees in camera, preventing scrutiny of how Parliament operates. It requires majority support to move a matter in camera; the members of the majority government caucus can, when convenient, vote to move a motion away from the prying eyes of the public and the media.

As well as moving inconvenient committee discussions in camera in order to avoid the glare of publicity, the government has also taken to attempting to control — to the point of preventing it — committee work that it takes exception to. At a Justice Committee meeting in the winter of 2013, the NDP justice critic put forward a perfectly reasonable motion, requiring that the committee conduct a study regarding a whistle-blower's allegation that the minister of justice was not vetting government legislation for Charter compliance before tabling the legislation, as required by statute.

This was, in my view, a serious allegation, especially given the growing number of the government's tough-on-crime bills that had been struck down by the courts for being in violation of some Charter-protected right. I was not satisfied by the assurance given me by the parliamentary secretary to the minister of justice that all proposed legislation was indeed being properly vetted. She described some vague process that was being followed, which did not seem particularly similar to the very specific process prescribed and allegedly not followed according to the whistle-blower's assertion.

However, the government, apparently not believing it was answerable to the committee, and certainly not to the NDP justice critic, instructed its majority on the committee to vote the motion down. Given the serious nature of the allegations, and since I was not feeling particularly compliant that day, I suggested that Ms. Boivin table her motion for forty hours (until the next meeting) to allow me to do my own research and allow the parliamentary secretary the opportunity to provide a more credible assurance that the government was, in fact, living up to its statutory Charter-vetting obligations.

I have never in my professional life caused such chaos or such a ruckus! Multiple staffers were literally running in and out of the committee room. Blackberries were buzzing constantly, as the executive staffers tried to figure out what the hell was going on. Did a backbencher just vote to hold over a motion potentially embarrassing to the justice minister rather than vote it down as instructed? This may have been precedent setting: a Conservative backbencher looking for assurance that the minister of justice was complying with the law!

The entire process concluded with an invitation to attend the principal's office (that is the office of the chief government whip). I was, not so subtly, reminded of the expectations of me as a member of the team. Shortly thereafter, I was transferred off of the Justice Committee, albeit largely for reasons unrelated to my above attempt to hold the government to account and in compliance with the law.

3. THE CAUCUS

I suppose that if there was a criticism of my performance as a member of the Conservative government caucus it was that I was not a team player. If my critics equate being a team player with being a government cheerleader, I concede the point.

Now, within caucus, there are obviously differing understandings of this role both in concept and in application. There are those who believe members, owing their election to the party and the party leader, are essentially an extension of the Prime Minister's Office Communications Branch. Proponents of this model believe it is the purpose of MPs to read prepared lines in the House and then return to the ridings on break weeks to continue the selling of the government's messaging. Any straying from approved communication lines is viewed as going rogue.

When I served as a Conservative MP, I took a more nuanced view of my role as a backbench caucus member. As a member of the government caucus, I was loyal to the party and to the leader, under whose banner I was elected. Accordingly, I felt obliged to support the government's legislative agenda and I believe my voting record reflected consistency in that regard. However, supporting the government does not, in my view, necessitate blindly and mindlessly supporting everything the government says or does.

In my view, the constructive criticism of government initiatives is not the equivalent of mutiny, or even disloyalty. Quite the opposite actually; sycophants and yes-men are certainly less valuable to a government's performance than constructive critics who demonstrate their loyalty by challenging the government to continually perform even better. Whereas a yes-man will continue to cheer blindly even as it becomes obvious that a policy is going off the rails, the constructive critic, not shy of speaking truth to power, will advise his caucus colleagues of the proposed policy's shortcomings in order that improvements can be made — changes that will ensure that the final policy is sound. In so doing, he demonstrates his loyalty to his party and his government.

Traditional caucus loyalists believe that all differences between caucus members ought to be resolved in caucus behind closed doors; once a position is determined, the party leaves the caucus room united and singing from a single song sheet. It all seems perfectly reasonable; however, as appealing as in camera discussions might be for those concerned only with the party's interests, they do absolutely nothing to promote the public interest. When a decision is under consideration behind closed doors, it is inevitable that political ramifications will also be under consideration. How will this initiative be viewed by the base? How will the voters react in the strategic swing ridings? How will the party's fundraising be affected?

These partisan considerations might be extremely important to party operatives, but they are of absolutely no relevance to the taxpaying constituents that a Member of Parliament is supposed to be representing. In order to ensure that it is the public's interests rather than the party's interests that are being considered, transparency demands that important matters be decided in public.

A public discussion of the issues would ensure that the points of view of the various stakeholders are heard and considered. Such is certainly not the case in a typical CPC caucus meeting, which in fact barely qualifies as a meeting. The process is completely controlled by the party leadership and more closely resembles a briefing than a meeting. There are no motions; there are no votes. There is no Roberts Rules of Order.

Caucus members do receive updates, and they hear from the prime minister how great they all are and how Canadians trust only them to manage the country, especially the economy. To remove any doubt, caucus members are provided talking points, canned stump speeches, and sample letters to the editors of local newspapers, all designed to reinforce the government's messaging and the caucus member's role in distributing those communications to his or her constituents.

Members are briefed about the government's plans and proposed legislative initiatives. However, these plans and initiatives are often news to the caucus members as, frequently, no notes will have been distributed in advance to provide background. That deficiency significantly compromises the caucus members' ability to ask researched or meaningful questions.

More problematic, no votes are ever taken inside the government caucus room. A minister will brief the caucus concerning a legislative initiative she intends to introduce. She will take questions and will attempt to provide clarification and satisfy concerns caucus members may have. But the government bill will not formally (or informally) be approved by the caucus. Caucus members will subsequently be whipped, or instructed, to support a bill or motion that they have had the opportunity to discuss but have never had the opportunity to approve.

An Opposition motion or bill will similarly be presented to the caucus. The government will state its position; there will be a discussion of it and the opportunity to ask questions. But no vote will ever take place. Caucus members will be expected to follow the government's position regarding the proposal but will never have the opportunity to ratify that government position.

This is very different from situation that existed in the provincial Progressive Conservative caucus of Ralph Klein, which I had the pleasure of serving in from 2001–2004. Premier Klein ran what at least approximated a democratic caucus. No legislative proposal could make it to the floor of the Alberta Legislature without first having been vetted, then supported by an actual vote at a standing policy committee of the caucus and finally by a show-of-hands vote at a full caucus meeting.

The party whip would ask for a show of hands on all matters before the caucus. If the result was not obvious, hands would remain up until a formal count could be taken. If a minister's recommendation was defeated, the minister could tweak the proposal or remedy the defect and bring it back for approval, but nothing made it onto the floor of the legislature without caucus approval.

I was able to use that democratic vetting process in 2003 to delay radical changes to Alberta's automobile insurance regime for over a year. In a well-publicized display of democracy in action, Finance Minister Pat Nelson had to modify her legislative proposals, which capped injury claims, several times. It was not until she changed the legislation to include public consultation and a mandatory legislative review in the future that the bill received the requisite caucus support and could proceed to First Reading in the Alberta Legislature.

There is no comparable vetting or approval process in the caucus of the Conservative Party of Canada. In a partial, but woefully inadequate, attempt to remedy this defect, the government established Caucus Advisory Committees (CACs) several years ago. The CACs are comprised of the caucus members who are assigned to various committees; other caucus members may attend, but the schedules are not published.

The aptly named *advisory* committees are briefed on imminent legislation initiatives and can ask questions and provide input. Informal votes are sometimes taken, but these are completely non-binding on the minister — a fact that perfectly illustrates the focus-group relevance of the CPC caucus including the CACs. For example, the Justice CAC unanimously approved salary disclosure, in PMB C-461 (also known as the CBC and Public Disclosure Act), at $188,000. However, the committee's approval of this bill did not prevent the executive from instructing the evisceration of the CBC and Public Disclosure Act at the Access and Ethics Committee. As with all other aspects of their role as members of that caucus, MPs are expected to willingly and unequivocally follow the will of the party leadership.

As a result, the government caucus plays no meaningful or substantive role in holding the government to account.

4. THE SENATE

On Tuesday, March 05, 2013, the House of Commons was debating an NDP Opposition day motion seeking to abolish the "chamber of sober second thought" (the Senate). They cited recent well-publicized allegations against specific senators as a rationale for mothballing the $92 million upper house. I listened intently to their argument, but was not remotely persuaded, save to the extent that recent developments reinforce the need to reform the Senate.

Firstly, every institution has members who have fallen beneath the standard expected of them. All professions — physicians, lawyers, businessmen, and clergy — have had members fall from grace; yet we do not abolish their important institutions. Members of Parliament and members of provincial legislatures, past and present, have been, and are, embroiled in ethical and even legal quagmires. In the end, senator misconduct is not a good argument in favour of Senate abolishment. The institution is bigger and more important than the individuals who comprise it.

Secondly, the Senate serves a useful, although frequently misunderstood, purpose. The Senate does in fact provide a deliberate and thoughtful second look at legislation that was inadequately vetted by the House of Commons. A recent example was PMB C-290, dealing with single-event sports betting. The bill seemed straightforward: it would allow casinos to take wagers on single games — currently they will only accept bets on multiple games, to prevent against game fixing, something that has become a problem in European football matches.

The House rushed the bill through, as it had bi-partisan support. At the Senate hearings, however, it was discovered that all the major professional sports associations were vehemently opposed to the legislation. Paul Beeston, president of the Toronto Blue Jays, went so far as to opine that expansion of minor league professional baseball in Canada would be compromised if the bill became law. The Senate correctly put the brakes on potentially damaging legislation until more information could be obtained and important questions answered.

Although unicameral legislatures do exist in modern democratic states, they are certainly the exception, not the norm. The democracies of Scandinavia, New Zealand, and Singapore all have single houses. But the United States and most Commonwealth countries have bicameral legislatures, designed specifically to provide checks and balances, allowing reconsideration of inadequately vetted legislation in a manner similar to the incident cited above where brakes were put on the gambling legislation.

Ironically, the Senate sometimes comes under attack for doing its job. In fact, the Senate usually comes under criticism when it actually amends legislation approved by the democratically elected House. Critics argue that an appointed body has no legitimacy in overriding an elected body. However, as we saw with the case of the single-sport betting bill, hastily approved by the House of Commons but opposed by all professional sports associations concerned by match fixing, the Senate attempted to improve the legislation and fulfilled its constitutional obligation by applying the brakes to the bill and ordering protracted study and hearings.

Constitutional experts cite the potential for gridlock between chambers and the slowing down of government reforms as negative bicameral side effects. The cynic in me suspects that is the real reason the NDP supports Senate abolition. If they ever form government, they might find the upper house unsympathetic to an aggressive socialist agenda.

The framers of the U.S. Constitution, in published papers, were most mistrustful of unencumbered power. Madison further warned of the "fickleness and passion that could absorb the House." Accordingly, they designed a system that separated the executive from the legislature and then further divided legislative powers into a House and a Senate. The drafters believed that the different houses would represent different interests. Whereas the British House of Lords was designed to represent the aristocracy, the U.S. Senate was designed to promote regional representation. Accordingly, the Constitution provided for two senators from every state of the Union with terms much longer than House members. Prior to the Seventeenth Amendment, the senators were actually appointed by the state legislatures, thus confirming their role in providing regional representation and safeguarding the states' rights.

Aspects of both models were incorporated into the Canadian Senate. The British North America Act provided property requirements for eligibility and allows the prime minister to appoint senators, similar to the appointment process for the House of Lords. But the Canadian Constitution also established that each region of Canada would have a specified number of individuals eligible to sit in the upper house. This is borrowed from the U.S. model and reflects the realities of diverse regional interests in a large geographic country such as Canada.

Regional representation is a legitimate priority. However, the Canadian Senate ceased to be a body of regional representation, if it ever was one, decades ago. In the U.S. Senate, senators will frequently break rank with their party to defend a matter of regional interest or protect the state they represent. This is natural, as they will eventually have to face the electorate again. Canadian senators abandon their loyalty to their province in favour of the party that appointed them immediately after having been sworn in. The Senate was designed to provide sober second thought, not to be a warehouse for party loyalists and bagmen.

Accordingly, the chamber needs to be reformed so that senators are elected and accountable to their constituents, not to the party that appointed them.

Defenders of liberty believe that the greatest threat is the concentration of power. The division of powers between the federal government and the provinces and the division of federal powers between bicameral legislatures are both part of a deliberate system of checks and balances to minimize the approval of ill-considered legislation. Parliament exists to hold government to account; an effective Senate is integral to that parliamentary prerogative.

I remain a strong proponent of bicameralism (two houses of parliament), provided that both houses are functional. The current PMO/Senate Expenses Scandal confirms my belief that our system needs more, not fewer, checks and balances on executive power. Bicameral legislatures exist to provide a further check on both government power and the lower house by providing "sober second thought" to the deliberations of the lower, and in Canada the only elected, legislative chamber.

I am also a strong proponent for Senate reform. Although the current problems facing the Senate underline the dysfunctional state of affairs that exists there at present and cause many to support abolition, that option should seriously be considered if, and only if, reform is impracticable. Given the constitutional realities, reform is indeed challenging; however, as abolition is subject to even more onerous constitutional considerations, we should probably be resigned to incremental reform being more likely than abolition.

Potentially, the Senate could have an important role to play in reconsidering legislation improperly vetted by the lower House. Admittedly, it would do so with much greater legitimacy if the senators were elected and therefore accountable to someone other than the political party that appointed them. However, until the Constitution is amended to provide for compulsory, rather than non-binding, advisory senatorial elections, the Constitution Act does in fact give equal status in the legislative process to the Senate as is enjoyed by the House.

Although the Senate was criticized for "gutting" Bill C-377, a trade union disclosure bill, by raising the disclosure threshold, it did not do so with anything close to finality. Amending the bill as the Senate did, parliamentary procedure ensured that the bill would be returned to the House of Commons for further debate and deliberation. It is only when a bill is passed by both chambers in identical form that it becomes law. The title bestowed on the Senate — the "Upper House" — is not descriptive of the the Senate's role in the legislative process.

Like the judicial branch of government, senators get their legitimacy from the Constitution and the fact they are not elected is immaterial from a legal perspective. However, the appointment process for the Senate is antiquated. It attempts to combine the House of Lords' concept of protecting landowners' rights with the American Senate's attempt at providing representation on a loosely defined regional basis. Only the latter — the defending of regional interests — remains of relevance in a country as large and geographically diverse as Canada. However, if appointed senators exercise more deference to the party that appointed them than to the region or province they represent, their usefulness is indeed questionable.

However, by breaking party rank occasionally, amending flawed private members' bills and sending them back to the House for further consideration, the Senate did indeed show its value in providing an important check on the House of Commons and in the process also showed that the tools for holding government to account exist should the senators choose to use them.

Amending the Constitution to either elect senators or abolish the entire institution is going to be difficult, if not impossible. Accordingly, any changes that result in a depoliticization of the chamber will effect a noticeable improvement. All too frequently, the Senate caucus is as disciplined and deferential to leadership as the House caucuses. More rubber stamping is unhelpful. Until we are in a position to have actual senatorial elections, democratic reformers will be limited to insisting that future appointments be based on merit, experience, policy expertise, or outstanding achievement in a chosen field.

The greatest factor in our democratic deficit is not the unelected Senate, but the ebbing of power away from Parliament and its concentration inside the Prime Minister's Office. However, a Senate operating as a PMO branch plant, as it has been recently, serves no purpose whatsoever. For a chamber to provide sober second thought, it must have some notional objectivity. A Senate full of partisan appointments and government cheerleaders provides the farthest thing from that objective standard.

Appointing senators based on the quality of the representation they might provide, rather than according to their partisan pedigree, will be an integral interim step to an eventual constitutional amendment providing for a fully elected Senate. Our broken democracy needs more and better-functioning checks on centralized power — not fewer.

5.

CABINET: A REPRESENTATIVE NOT A DELIBERATIVE BODY

I grew up in Melville, Saskatchewan, and have always had an interest in local history. Once I became a parliamentarian, I decided to research Melville's political history.

For almost a half-century, Melville was represented by two high-profile Liberal MPs, both of whom served in the federal cabinet as the minister of agriculture. The second, elected during the Second World War, was former Saskatchewan premier Jimmy Gardiner. His predecessor was a homesteader from the Abernethy district named W.R. Motherwell.

Motherwell was initially elected to represent the riding of Regina. But due to electoral redistribution, Motherwell decided to contest the riding of Melville, for which he was elected to the 16th Parliament on September 14, 1926. However, he promptly resigned the seat on October 11, forcing a by-election for Melville, in which Motherwell was acclaimed on November 2, 1926.

Why were there two elections in six weeks?

According to the Parliament of Canada's records, Motherwell's resignation from the House of Commons was necessary because of his "acceptance of [an] emolument under the Crown." An emolument is simply a salary, fee, or profit from employment or an office. So, Motherwell received employment from the federal Crown necessitating his resignation from Parliament.

What was the federal appointment that constituted a conflict with his role as a member of a Parliament which he was elected to less than a month prior?

On October 11, 1926, Prime Minister Mackenzie King appointed Motherwell to his cabinet as minister of agriculture. The acceptance of this emolument under the Crown necessitated that Motherwell resign his recently acquired seat in the House of Commons. The seemingly strange convention of the day was that a newly appointed minister had to resubmit his candidacy to his constituents in a by-election to determine if he still had their support. And so, Motherwell was forced to resign his seat and run again. He did so and was re-elected.

Today, it would appear inconceivable that a riding would not want to be represented by a powerful cabinet minister. But this interesting parliamentary anecdote is an important reminder of the distinction and potential conflict that exists between being a member of the legislature and being a member of the executive government.

The House of Commons was created to represent and defend the English commoners from the excessive demands and needs of the Crown. The monarch would have to submit his request for taxes to the House of Commons. The House existed to ensure that the king's requests were reasonable and that the taxpayers were not overly burdened.

The House exists to represent the citizens who elect it. The executive government was disassociated from the elected Parliament. As a result, an MP asked to sit as a cabinet minister would have conflicting roles, a situation requiring him to seek reconfirmation of his legislative role from his constituents.

Remember from Chapter 2 that in British North America the governor in the colonies was appointed by Great Britain; thereafter, the governor appointed his executive council. However, the emolument rule prohibited members of the legislature from becoming cabinet ministers unless and until they resigned and then were re-elected in a by-election. The maintenance of this convention was an express attempt to reduce British executive influence in the legislatures of Upper and Lower Canada (which would later become Ontario and Quebec). This convention was carried on and codified after Confederation by the act appropriately named The Independence of Parliament Act, 1867.

This rule, maintained until 1931, members of the Canadian House of Commons were prohibited from serving as cabinet ministers, unless and until they resigned and then were re-elected in a by-election. The convention was an express attempt to reduce British executive influence in the legislatures of Upper and Lower Canada. (Remember from Chapter 2 that the governor in the Colonies was appointed by Great Britain and thereafter, the governor appointed his executive council.)

This convention was carried on and codified after Confederation by the act appropriately named "The Independence of Parliament Act, 1867."

Accordingly, this convention, then codified in statute, represented an attempt to manage the inherent conflict that exists between the ministers of the executive, who spend money appropriated to it by the legislative branch, and the legislative branch itself. It was thought that perhaps the taxpayers in a riding might prefer to be represented by a legislator who was a fiscal hawk rather than by a free-spending minister. Accordingly, that question was put to them in a by-election.

Followers of American politics understand this concept, and conflict, as the American Constitution establishes a complete separation of powers between the legislative and executive branches. Accordingly, Barack Obama had to resign his Senate seat upon being elected president, and Hillary Clinton and John Kerry both had to do likewise on being called as successive Secretaries of State.

❖

In Canada, becoming a cabinet minister is the pinnacle of career advancement for most MPs. Cabinet ministers are referred to by a variety of monikers: Minister, Honourable, Privy Councillor, and member of the executive council. However, despite these grand-sounding titles, the reality is that the importance of the position has continually declined as more and more power is concentrated in the Prime Minister's Office.

The decline in ministerial input inside the Ottawa Bubble has been evolving for nearly a half-century and has been commensurate with the growth in size of government and in the size of the cabinet itself. Originally, the Canadian cabinet consisted of twelve ministers. The number of members has ballooned since then. Brian Mulroney had the largest Canadian cabinet with forty ministers. In July 2013, Prime Minister Stephen Harper increased the size of his cabinet to thirty-nine. Add thirty-one parliamentary secretaries, who are not currently sworn to the Privy Council but serve an executive function (in that they answer for the government in the House in the absence of their respective minister), and the current executive numbers seventy. With a caucus of approximately 160 members, the odds of an MP eventually being promoted to the executive are better than one in three. When one adds the positions of committee chairs and vice chairs, which also come with an emolument, the odds improve to almost one in two. Clearly, the odds of reaching the executive ranks are pretty good for loyal soldiers, i.e., those who serve the interests of the executive rather than hold that executive to account.

Over time, increasingly large cabinets have proven themselves too unwieldy. Anyone who has ever tried to have a board meeting with thirty-nine people seated at the table appreciates the frustration. Decision-making requires units of a workable size, and as a result, a secretariat and cabinet committee system have developed. The secretariat for the cabinet and its committees is provided by the Privy Council Office, which reports to the prime minister.

The most powerful cabinet committees are the Treasury Board and the Priorities and Planning Committee of Cabinet. Senior non-elected public servants participate in cabinet committee meetings but are generally excluded from actual cabinet meetings. Given the increased size of the cabinet, the reliance on committees attended by senior public servants has facilitated the transfer of power from the cabinet to the Privy Council Office and the Prime Minister's Office.

There is rarely a more anticipated event in Ottawa then the day a new cabinet is unveiled at Rideau Hall. However, it is becoming increasingly apparent that in choosing a ministry the first minister is cognizant of many factors unrelated to merit. Every region, and ideally every province, requires representation. Linguistic and ethnic considerations are also taken into account. The number of women in cabinet is important as is the number of francophone individuals; Aboriginal representation and the presence of visible minorities are all matters of great interest to those respective communities. Given the desire to include as diverse a group as possible around the cabinet table, it is hardly surprising that talent is not always the most prominent consideration and that cabinets have grown dramatically in size.

Compare how Canada's government is chosen to how Canada's national hockey team is chosen. On January 7, 2014, Hockey Canada announced the lineup for the 2014 men's Olympic hockey team. Not a single member of the Edmonton Oilers, Calgary Flames, or Toronto Maple Leafs was named to the roster. This choice stands in marked contrast to that made for the All-Star team, where great care is taken to attempt to assure that all NHL teams have at least one representative. Of course, the NHL All-Star game is a show game — there is no hitting and little defence, it's just a glitzy performance. In contrast, the Olympic hockey team represents the best of Canadian hockey, with its members chosen on the basis of merit and individual talent and the contribution a member can bring to the team. At the Olympics, a gold medal is on the line; the All-Star game is mostly for show.

For those in charge of the political system, a Canadian cabinet will ideally be a microcosm of Canadian society, with as many identifiable groups as possible represented. This priority has been the largest contributing factor to the increase in the size of Canadian cabinets. A survey of the current Canadian ministry will reveal ministers of Chinese, Sikh, Métis, and Inuit backgrounds. Meanwhile, there are parliamentary secretaries who hail from the South Asian, African, Taiwanese and Greek communities.

Although Canada's government is becoming more inclusive, this reality reinforces the ever-decreasing significance of the cabinet and the merit of those chosen to sit inside it. As power has been continually transferred from the cabinet to cabinet committees and from those to the PMO, the quality of cabinet ministers has come to matter less and less. Identity has become more important than talent, and so there has been a general decline in the latter — a decline proportionate to the cabinet's diminishing influence.

In recent years, cabinets, ceasing to be deliberative bodies, have become increasingly merely ornamental. The members are chosen because of the demographic they represent and their role is reduced to the equivalent of the prime minister's cipher. The growing trend is to have policies, priorities, legislative initiatives, and even budgetary plans developed in the Prime Minister's Office and by its unelected staffers. The cabinet has, for some time now, been a representative body not dissimilar to an NHL All-Star team, existing largely for show, but devoid of the power and significance it once had and still deserves.

❖

The growing imbalance between the legislative and executive branches of government is exacerbated by the use of the government's discretionary power, allowing the cabinet to govern by Order-in-Council or by ministerial order. These are delegated powers, authorized by statute, which allow the cabinet to govern by regulation, authorized by the cabinet but never ratified by Parliament (which authorized the delegated authority in the statute).

Not only is Parliament being effectively bypassed as a result of rule by decree, cabinet is also being shut out of the decision-making process. Observers and former ministers confirm that PMO decisions and plans are distributed at cabinet meetings for perfunctory approval or rubber stamping. In the current Harper government, many minsters are unable to speak to the media or make departmental announcements without first having the communication cleared by the minions inside the Prime Minister's Office. A minister who cannot hire or fire either his chief of staff or his deputy minister is less a head of a government department than a conduit between the PMO and the department.

So diluted is the role and efficacy of the individual cabinet minister now that the time-honoured convention of ministerial responsibility has all but disappeared. Under responsible government, all ministers are jointly responsible for the decisions of the entire government and each minister is responsible for the performance of his or her individual department.

Accordingly, a minister of the Crown must resign from cabinet if he cannot publically support a decision of the government. The last time this occurred was in 2006, when Michael Chong resigned his cabinet seat over a disagreement with the prime minister about declaring Quebec a nation within Canada. This was proper and honourable, and it is perhaps the last time we will ever see it.

More recently, we have witnessed the senior minister from Quebec, Denis Lebel, publically endorse the then government of Quebec's position regarding separation — that a bare majority (50 percent + 1) of support is all that is required to allow Quebec to commence proceedings to put Canada asunder.[1] This is in contrast with the official policy of the Government of Canada, which mandates that a "clear majority on a clear question" is a prerequisite for commencing separation proceedings. However, Minister Lebel faced no sanctions or discipline.

Most ministers do not openly challenge the government's position. However, it has become common practice for ministers who are opposed to its position on a matter to absent themselves from a vote in the House, rather than resign from the cabinet or support the government's position despite their opposition. This was quite apparent during the vote on C-377, a bill dealing with trade union disclosure (this bill would, ironically, have made trade unions much more transparent than the federal government). Several ministers, who saw either the hypocrisy or the inconsistent application of this proposal, including the then–minister of natural resources and the associate minister of defence, left the Commons just prior to the recorded vote.

Then there are the many ministerial mistakes and misdeeds for which there is no longer any accounting. Historically, a finance minister who attempted to intervene or even speculate on financial markets would find himself in breach of sworn duty. However, the current government's preoccupation with politicizing everything has allowed the late Jim Flaherty to speculate that interest rates would rise and that the Canadian dollar would decline in value.[2] These comments not only raised confusion and action inside financial markets, they also raised concerns about the independence of the Bank of Canada. However, the government defended these actions. So, we should not be surprised when some former minister lobbies Bay Street bankers not to lower interest rates or allow certain groups to take on more household debt.

Not only are such misdeeds free from repercussions, colossal screw-ups within departments have also not resulted in ministers tendering their resignations. Underestimating the cost of CF-35s by over $30 billion (over 300 percent), gross losses of Canadians' personal information, and diverting millions of dollars earmarked for security to pay for tourist gazebos in the minister's own riding should have, but did not, cost the minister responsible his or her job.

And even apparent, overt acts of malfeasance escape the taking of any ministerial responsibility let alone ministerial resignation. When the word "not" is inserted before the word "recommended" on a CIDA funding document, or when a minister uses a military helicopter to pick him up from a private fishing vacation and deliver him to a government funding announcement, the offending minister should have earned an exit from the cabinet. However, nothing happened. I suppose that it is difficult to hold the minister responsible when he or she is merely carrying out the wishes or orders of the Prime Minister's Office.

It appears that negligent operation of a file, negligent supervision of a department, needless meddling, and even malfeasance no longer have any real consequences for cabinet ministers. Ministerial responsibility has been replaced by rationalization of one's actions and conduct. Rationalization and spin is all that is required in the eyes of the government … as long as, but only as long as, the minister has the support of the Prime Minister's Office.

And what, besides representing a particular demographic, determines if a cabinet minister is worth supporting and defending in the all-important viewpoint of the Prime Minister's Office?

Once somebody becomes a political liability, under the bus he goes. But as long as he can effectively communicate the government's message, and any foibles or problems can be handled with spin, the minister is considered a valued member of the team. In fact, effective communications skills have displaced superior management and leadership skills as the qualities of primary importance, as the cabinet has been reduced to the most important asset in the government's communications arsenal.

It is the difference between statesmanship and salesmanship. A statesman will tell you the truth; a salesman will tell you want you want to hear. A statesman will acknowledge good points in opponents and their arguments. A salesman will embellish the product he is trying to sell and be dismissive of alternatives. A statesman will point out both sides of an argument; a salesman will show you the beautiful backyard and hope you don't notice the cracks in the foundation. A statesman will tell you how much it will cost to fix the faulty foundation. A salesman will try to convince you can fix it with silicon filler and a coat of paint.

We have far too many salesman and far too few statesmen amongst our political elites. But if you accept the premise that even the cabinet ministers are largely removed from a centrally controlled decision-making structure, it is clear that there is no other role for them other than that of pitchman for their bosses at the PMO.

Notable exceptions exist, but the predominant role of the present-day Canadian cabinet minister is less that of policy maker and administrator than party loyalist and front-line communications messenger. To the list of ministerial monikers (Minister, Honourable, Privy Councillor) should also be added the rapidly developing predominant role of "Communister."

6.

PARTY DISCIPLINE: YOU ARE THERE TO SUPPORT THE TEAM

In one of my favourite episodes of my favourite sitcom *Seinfeld*, Jerry comes into possession of four playoff hockey tickets for a game between the New York Rangers and the New Jersey Devils. With George taking a pass on the game to impress a new girlfriend, Elaine asks her Devils fan boyfriend, David Putty, to attend. However, when they are getting ready to leave, Elaine discovers that her enthusiastic hockey fan date has painted his face in the colours of the Devils — bright red and green.

When she asks the face painter why he looks as he does, Putty replies with eyes squinted, "You gotta support the team."

An incredulous Elaine exclaims, "Well you can't go out looking like that."

Undeterred and unfazed, Putty inquires, "Why not?"

Exasperated, Elaine replies, "Because it's insane!"

David Putty would make a great and valued member of the Conservative Party of Canada, or any other House of Commons caucus. Indeed, for modern Canadian caucuses, loyalty to the team and a desire to impress teammates and leaders are not only valued qualities, they are qualities that are seemingly valued above all others. Blind loyalty is valued over constructive criticism, and certainly over the ability to speak truth to power. These realities are certainly beneficial for promoting team and caucus solidarity. They have a negative effect, however, on an individual MP's self-esteem and are ultimately detrimental to both democracy and to good decision-making.

I have previously stated, somewhat famously, that back-benchers of the governing party like to think of themselves as part of the government. They are not.[1] Under our constitutional convention of responsible government, the executive is accountable to the legislature. But the executive is not the legislative caucus of the governing party. The executive is the prime minister and his handpicked ministers of the Crown. Each minister heads, and is responsible for, a department of the permanent government bureaucracy. Since parliamentary secretaries answer questions in the House when their minister is absent and are frequently dispatched to the cable political news shows to defend the government, PSs must, by extension, be deemed to be part of the executive/government. However, the rest of the legislative caucus of the governing party is not part of the government. As MPs, their role should be to serve their constituents by holding the government to account. In theory this could involve occasionally voting against the government.

The government (ministers and parliamentary secretaries) are bound by two-line whips (instructions from party leadership) during votes. However, backbenchers, at least theoretically, are supposed to be allowed to vote independently on all but three-line whips. The convention of cabinet solidarity requires that a minister (or parliamentary secretary) must always support the government position when voting, or in public, or resign from his or her position. No similar doctrine of caucus solidarity exists, although an imposed one has been rapidly evolving.

I am always amused when Conservative backbenchers refer to "our government." Again, backbenchers are not part of the government. However, sitting in the Commons, one frequently hears a member's statement that begins, "Mr. Speaker, our government's number one priority is job creation," or something similar. Equally common are planted questions, delivered during Question Period, that begin with the same premise. A question such as, "Can the Minister of Finance comment on our government's recent positive employment statistics?" is founded on the same false premise: that a backbench MP from the governing party is part of the government.

Even more troubling than these statements and questions, though, is the practice of Conservative backbenchers attending photo opportunities that are masquerading as government funding announcements, occasionally with novelty oversized cheques. "Our government is pleased to support the community through this important investment in infrastructure," the backbencher will proclaim. The necessary implication, conveyed to the local media, is that the local MP was somehow responsible for obtaining the investment for his constituents. The reality is that the decision was made by a bureaucrat and then approved by a regional minister, both of whom are part of the government, which the announcing MP is not.

An interesting aside: I am no longer involved in making government funding announcements, even within the boundaries of my riding, Edmonton-St. Albert. It has been deemed more "appropriate" that a Conservative MP from a neighbouring constituency make the announcement. This is a blatant attempt by the government to indulge in partisan advertising using public tax dollars; the appreciative recipients of the funding announcement are supposed to believe that the grant came from the Conservative government (or the Harper government, as it is more often termed), when the reality is that the funds are courtesy of the *Canadian* government.

❖

Two very odd and symbiotic sociological trends help to foster the belief in the desirability and necessity of this "team playership." The first is the desire, sometimes the need, to belong. I cannot adequately explain why members of caucus place such emphasis on the importance of being part of the team. Perhaps it is the isolation and loneliness of being marooned in Ottawa and away from family and friends for half of the calendar year. Maybe it is the constant reminders from party leadership that politicians win as a team and they lose as a team. Ralph Klein frequently would borrow a hockey analogy and remind his caucus that you play for the logo on the front of the sweater and not the name on the back. Whatever the reason or combination of factors at play, there is great emphasis on the notion that "you gotta support the team."

The second factor is that the party leadership unequivocally encourages all members and supporters of the government to think of themselves as members of the team. You would think that ego and arrogance would result in leaders and ministers regarding their governmental club with some sense of exclusivity. However, just the opposite is true. Why?

It serves the interests of the leadership to have all caucus members, and, in fact, all party members, think of themselves as part of, and contributing to, the team. Caucus members are more likely to defend the government's record and party messaging, and donors are more likely to send the party financial support if they are made to feel that they are a part of it all.

The feeling of being part of a team is particularly stressed at weekly caucus meetings. Every caucus meeting begins and ends with an address by the leader. The opening comments are generally mundane: a summary of relevant events which occurred since the caucus last met and/or the plans regarding the week(s) ahead. However, the closing comments, which are akin to a half-time pep talk, would make a college football coach proud. After summarizing the government's record, Prime Minister Harper will close a Wednesday caucus meeting with a Knute Rockne-esque speech including platitudes, such as: "Now let's go back to our ridings this weekend and remind Canadians that we are the only ones they trust to manage the economy; and that we are the only party with ideas for the economic growth and crime prevention that Canadians want and deserve." "And now let's go win one for the Gipper," would not seem out of place!

So pervasive is this emphasis on the team and players that in the spring of 2013, during the so-called "backbench spring," Chief Government Whip Gordon O'Conner took the team analogy to new and disturbing limits. Langley MP Mark Warawa wished to deliver a statement in the House of Commons, expressing his disappointment that his private member's motion condemning gendercide would not be allowed to proceed to a debate. O'Connor justified denying Warawa the opportunity to speak in the House by stating that the caucus was a team and that he was the coach. As coach, he argued, he had the unfettered discretion to determine who gets to "play."[2]

The problem is that governing a country is not a game. The stakes are much too high and the outcomes too important to trivialize them to the equivalent of a game. The bigger problem is that the inappropriateness of the analogy was clearly lost on the chief government whip. The sad reality is that government advisors too frequently will evaluate the success of any initiative, or the day's events, in terms of partisan objectives, rather than policy outcomes. But governing has to be more important than just notional winning; it ought to be about achieving effective outcomes for Canadians.

Although the Speaker's Ruling on the Warawa matter confirmed that only the Speaker ultimately gets to determine who is allowed to speak in the House of Commons, the reality is that backbenchers continue to allow themselves to be ruled by the government, believing that they are part of the government team. Because said belief serves the interest of the party leadership, it is in leadership's interest to ensure the team concept remains a powerful reality. In such political ecosystems, perception easily becomes reality. In such political ecosystems, there are rarely any occasions when the government needs to worry about restraining its backbench MPs — the members restrain themselves.

I have participated in four elections and close to twenty election forums. In almost every one of these job auditions, the question is posed: "How will the candidate, if successful, vote on a matter of local importance, if the position of the constituents is different than the official position of the party under whose banner the candidate is running?"

Invariably, the answer offered, especially by neophyte candidates, is, "Of course I will stand up for my local constituents." Incumbent candidates and those with more experience will offer a more nuanced answer, such as "it depends on the issue," or "you have to pick your battles and your hill to die on."

The truthful answer should probably be something along the lines of: "I will support the party position and thereafter attempt to persuade you of the correctness of that position, because if I stray from the party position, I will be out of the caucus and off the team and I can do more for you inside the caucus than I can from outside the tent."

I cannot recall how many times I have heard elected members defend their refusal to fight against a particular decision that the government has made to which they object, rationalizing that you have to pick your battles and choose your hill to die on. However, the reality is that the longer one has been part of the team, the easier the members find it to rationalize their decision to stay on the team as opposed to staying true to the principles that they truly believe in and that sent the member to Ottawa in the first place.

Notable exceptions exist. In the current Parliament, NDP MPs Bruce Hyer and John Rafferty, both rural Ontario MPs, split with their party leadership on the merits of the Long-Gun Registry and voted in support of a government bill to repeal it. Both faced internal discipline. As a result, Hyer left the NDP and sat as an Independent before eventually joining the Green Party caucus.

Another defender of principle over team is former Nova Scotia Conservative MP Bill Casey. Casey actually voted against a Conservative government budget in 2007, because the budget messed with the equalization formula and, allegedly, broke the Atlantic Accord. Casey voted against the budget and was expelled from the Conservative caucus mere minutes thereafter. However, so appreciative were Casey's Cumberland-Colchester constituents that they re-elected him with an impressive plurality when he ran as an Independent in the 2008 general election.

Teams and parties all use the aforementioned discipline to enforce loyalty to the team. When Hyer and Rafferty voted in favour of scrapping the Long-Gun Registry, they were removed from their respective committee assignments, disallowed from speaking in the House of Commons (as the whips had complete control of the speaking lists pre-Warawa), and suspended from all international parliamentary travel (junkets).

In the fall of 2012, the Conservative party leadership tried to discipline me when I refused to remove, or edit, several blog posts I had written that were critical of such non-conservative matters as ministerial opulence (e.g., expense claims for such things as $16 glasses of orange juice and parliamentary limousines), the F-35 fighter jet procurement fiasco, and taxpayer subsidies to private corporations.

Now, party discipline is truly medieval. It consists of a highly unsophisticated series of awards and punishments. Favourable committee assignments, office locations, and international parliamentary travel are held out as carrots. The stick is the threat to deny them.

When my blogging was deemed offside and I refused to delete or edit my posts I was removed from the Public Safety Committee and placed on the Library of Parliament Committee. My seat in the House of Commons was also moved, to the back corner of the Opposition side of the House.

The whip knew I coveted the Public Safety Committee, while the Library of Parliament Committee is famous for being the equivalent of a high-school detention hall. The irony was that being transferred from the Public Safety Committee to the Library of Parliament Committee was absolutely no punishment at all. Although the work of the Public Safety Committee is certainly more interesting and is better suited to my background as a lawyer, it also has a heavy workload. It sits a minimum of four hours per week and requires considerable reading and preparation time in advance of those meetings. The Library of Parliament Committee, meanwhile, almost never meets. It meets only once or twice per parliamentary session, sometimes only to elect a chair. Because it is a joint committee of Parliament, it always meets in an opulent room in the Senate's East Block, always at noon, and always with a hot lunch.

If they had really wanted to prevent me from blogging, they should have given me more, not less, work to do. They should have assigned me an extra busy committee, not taken one away. However, such is the medieval system of human-resource management inside the Ottawa Bubble.

I suspect that the powers that be actually believe that a recalcitrant team member will be so embarrassed or so ardently miss being a team player that he will eventually come around, regardless of how ineffective or counterintuitive the punishment is. And that does seem to be the case. As Andrew Coyne of Postmedia has correctly pointed out, the reason that party discipline is so effective is because it is largely self-imposed.[3] So strong is the need to be a member of the team that the team polices itself. Team members will occasionally feel the need to encourage players who have been tempted to stray from the pack to get back in line. More often, however, such action is unnecessary; the members exercise self-discipline entirely of their own volition.

The big carrots in the Ottawa Bubble are not international travel or a big office in the new Promenade Building. The big carrot is the upward or, more accurately, forward movement of one's political career. The prospect of moving from the back to the middle, and then, possibly, the front benches; the prospect of being named a committee chair, a parliamentary secretary, or, the brass ring, a cabinet minister — that is really the glue that makes party discipline stick.

Forward bench mobility means that MPs will generally impose discipline upon themselves. The more ambitious a member is, the more that he or she will be prepared to do to support the team. Attending party fundraisers and working by-elections is the minimum expected of a member. The more forwardly mobile will send attack 10-percenters (party messaging) into their ridings, read inane talking points rather than participate in an actual debate in the House of Commons, and go on cable political panels to defend the indefensible.

During the infamous Senator Duffy-Nigel Wright debacle, a forwardly mobile Parliament secretary told CBC's Evan Solomon that the then–chief of staff of the PMO was a Canadian patriot, so concerned that the taxpayers of Canada would be out the $90,000 that the senator had improperly claimed as a housing expense that he reached into his own pocket to ensure that the taxpayers would not be left holding the bag.

Four days later, Wright was gone, immediately becoming the object of vilification. Two months later, the aforementioned parliamentary secretary was appointed minister of state for democratic reform. This observation is in no way personal to the honourable minster, who I consider to be a friend; it is an institutional observation. The system, by design, encourages and promotes sycophancy. Prove yourself to be a loyal team player and your career prospects brighten. Represent your constituents and speak or vote in a different direction than your party leadership wishes you to and you will find yourself on the outside looking in.

American satirist P.J. O'Rourke wrote an entire treatise on this concept, aptly named *Parliament of Whores*.[4] No self-respecting individual would barter away his or her integrity or credibility in exchange for career advancement, especially in such an ephemeral world as Canadian politics. Just as no self-respecting adult would paint his face just to show support for his favourite hockey team. As Elaine Benes said in *Seinfeld*: "Because it's insane!"

7.

THE PRIME MINISTER:
THE AMERICANIZATION OF
CANADIAN POLITICS

The Canadian and American systems of government are very different. Although both, at least theoretically, are functioning democracies, the framers of the American Constitution rejected the Westminster style of parliamentary democracy in favour of a republic with a formal separation of powers. Whereas no member of the U.S. Congress can serve in the executive (both Barrack Obama and Hillary Clinton had to resign their Senate seats in 2008 to serve in the executive branch of government), it is almost unheard of, although constitutionally permissible, for a minister of the Crown not to be a member of the legislative branch.

Responsible government, by practical definition, ensures that the executive cabinet is comprised of, but distinguishable from, elected legislators. This fusion of the roles ensures a very powerful and dominant position in the job of Canadian prime minister.

A prime minister is both the head of the executive government and his party's chief spokesperson in the legislature. Given his predominant position in both the executive and legislative branches, he has no equal in a congressional system based on a separation of powers.

As noted earlier, eminent constitutional expert Peter Russell has remarked that to be a prime minister in a majority Parliament is like being a U.S. President without a Congress.[1] There are few practical checks on prime ministerial power and certainly none of them are housed in the Parliament Buildings.

A prime minister, supported by a caucus that holds a majority of seats in the House of Commons, is, if he chooses to be, an elected dictator for the duration of that Parliament. His government's agenda will find no opposition in the House of Commons; private members' bills and Opposition motions, meanwhile, will pass only if they receive the thumbs up from the PMO.

As we have seen recently, even the unelected Senate is not immune to the PMO's influence and attempts at control. Realistically, a prime minister who has appointed over half of all sitting senators is unlikely to find any checks and balances in the house of sober second thought either.

A prime minister's authority is further consolidated by his seemingly unfettered power of appointment. The governor-general-in-council, the constitutional term for the cabinet, appoints all senators, all superior court judges, including those appointed to all appellate courts and the Supreme Court of Canada. The prime minister formally appoints all members of his cabinet and the parliamentary secretaries to approximately half of the ministers. The cabinet then appoints the heads of all Crown corporations, the chairs and members of all government boards and commissions, all deputy ministers, all ambassadors, and all of the officers of Parliament, such as the auditor general, the chief electoral officer, and the privacy and ethics commissioners. Finally, the prime minister appoints or delegates the appointment of all members of the Prime Minister's Office and the Privy Council Office.

The prime minister may not be the head of state, but the U.S. president, who is head of state and shares responsibility for many of the above appointments, must have many of those appointments ratified by the U.S. Congress. A Canadian prime minister's power of appointment is subject to no comparable legislative ratification, although officers of Parliament are perfunctorily approved by the assembly.

As a result, the office of the prime minister is all important and dwarfs the importance of all supportive and secondary offices and positions. The late Jim Travers, in an excellent essay, remarked: "It is his clear and credible view that between elections, prime ministers now operate in the omnipotent manner of kings. Surrounded by subservient cabinet barons, fawning unelected courtiers and answerable to no one, they manage the affairs of state more or less as they please."[2]

This has even been demonstrated in the nomenclature of government communications. The current government is fond of referring to itself as the "Harper Government" in government communications and press releases, as opposed to the more familiar and, I would suggest, appropriate, "Government of Canada."

This trend has evolved to the point that election campaigns are almost exclusively leader driven. Whereas the media will travel thousands of kilometres covering the respective leaders' tours, the rest of the candidates will go largely unnoticed unless they fall prey to a gaffe or blunder.

Undoubtedly, the best predictor of the results in any constituency election is the popularity and effectiveness of the campaign of the leader under whose banner the candidate is running. Elections are determined largely on voters' impressions of national leaders, gleaned from national media sources. Many pundits and strategists believe that over 90 percent of the electorate make their voting decision based on some combination of their impression of the party and the party leader.

It has been suggested, sarcastically, that the candidate is a hood ornament in the election campaign, making a difference perhaps in a close electoral contest. How else do you explain the fact that several NDP candidates were elected in the Jack Layton "Orange Wave" without spending a dollar on the campaign and some not ever having been to their riding?

I understand this concept quite well. In the 2001 Alberta election, I was a replacement candidate. Nominated literally days before the writ was dropped, poorly organized, and not well financed, I was given little chance of successfully carrying the PC colours in 2001. However, in that election, Edmonton, for the first and, to some extent, only time, warmed up to Ralph Klein. His coattails were wide enough to provide me with a five-hundred-vote plurality in Edmonton-Calder.

However, by 2004, Edmonton had again turned on Premier Klein. Many long-time Capital Region MLAs went down to defeat, and despite the fact that many media commentators and constituents rated me as an effective representative, I was defeated in another three-way horse race. Ralph Klein's coattails carried me into the Alberta Legislature and they carried me out again three and a half years later.

Our elections are so leader-centric that most Canadians believe they directly elect their prime ministers and premiers. Of course, we do not; each of us elect a Member of Parliament and a member of the legislative assembly. It is the support that the respective party leaders enjoy amongst those legislators that will ultimately determine who has the confidence of the House and therefore can serve as first minister.

Meanwhile, MPs, who should understand that the prime minister is chosen based on the support they command in the House, play right into the Americanization of our polity by becoming "invisible." Compliant and loyal MPs are invisible in the sense that they become indistinguishable from their party and their party leadership. They worship at the altar of their leader in weekly caucus meetings and praise the leader's successes and downplay his or her failures in between. MPs have transformed themselves into servants of the leader rather than serving as a check on the leader's authority and a constructive critic of his or her policies.

This eventually becomes a vicious circle: with MPs indistinguishable from their party leadership, it is natural that the electorate will make a voting decision based almost exclusively on their feelings regarding the party leader.

It is perhaps because many Canadians erroneously believe that they directly elect the prime minister that they are so tolerant of the consolidation of near ultimate power inside that office. But in a functional democracy, we would not witness such an increasing concentration of power and control. Nor should we tolerate such limited accountability or lack of transparency.

Power and control are increasingly concentrated, and accountability is practised more often in theory than in reality. Pierre Trudeau once famously referred to Members of Parliament as nobodies and Stephen Harper told the *National Post* in 1998 that "the average backbench MP is little more than a benchwarmer for his or her political party."[3] That level of condescension would more appropriately be found in monarchs than in democratic leaders.

❖

In the last half century, successive prime ministers have gradually, but inexorably, consolidated power in the "centre." They have freed themselves from the restraints that once bound them to the voters, Parliament, cabinet, and even their political parties. All institutional checks on prime ministerial power are compromised, strained, and breaking, if not broken.

This situation is a long way from what was envisioned by the democratic reformers who fought for responsible government in the 1830s and 1840s. They rejected the idea of a Family Compact or ruling aristocratic elite. Similarly, the Fathers of Confederation rejected a presidential system of government. Instead, they opted for a Westminster model, where the prime minister would be accountable to a democratically elected legislature, not the lord over it. The degeneration of that system to one where the prime minister is subject to no effective checks or balances has been a slow process, and it is one that will be difficult to reverse.

It is clearly easy, as many MPs do, to support the status quo and ignore the system's obvious deficiencies. However, others recognize that our democracy is at a precipice and have taken measures to try to redress the imbalance between the power of the party leaders and their parties, and between appointed prime ministers and elected Parliaments.

An important initiative to rebalance the relationship between a party leader and his or her political party, and by logical extension the relationship between the prime minister and

Parliament, was tabled on December 3, 2013. The Reform Act 2013,[4] if adopted, will be a game changer. It will, to some extent, restore an appropriate balance to the Westminster model of Parliament as it exists in Canada. It will promote responsible government by making the prime minister accountable to a parliamentary caucus, not the master over it.

The Reform Act 2013, if passed, will establish three mechanisms common in the British parliamentary system of government, but conspicuously absent from the current Canadian adaptation.

The bill, introduced by Wellington-Halton Hills MP Michael Chong, will amend the Elections Act to take away the much maligned section of the act that mandates that a party leader sign the nomination papers of prospective candidates. This early Trudeau-era amendment to our election laws fundamentally altered the relationship between riding associations and their candidates or representatives, and, more damaging to our democratic institutions, the relationship between a party leader and his or her caucus.

The requirement that the nomination papers of a prospective candidate be signed by the party leader gives the leader a veto over nominations and removes the local riding association's ability, and therefore the local membership's ability, to pick a candidate of their choosing. Worse, it irrevocably alters the relationship between the leader and the caucus member. An incumbent member who falls out of favour with his party leadership will be prevented from seeking re-election.

This is not a hypothetical threat. Challenging authority or at least questioning it is fundamental to democracy, but for MPs tempted to do so the nuclear threat of losing the leader's endorsement may be the most efficacious means of keeping caucus members in line. Removing the necessity of the leader's endorsement rebalances democracy by making local candidates accountable to the riding association and their constituents, not the party establishment.

Secondly, the legislation will allow a caucus to implement a leadership review upon a petition of 15 percent of the elected members and a secret ballot vote garnering over 50 percent support.[*] A caucus's ability to fire the leader makes the leader accountable to the elected caucus; in contrast, in the current system elected members are little more than toadies, a focus group for their respective leaders.

The existing system, where party leaders are elected at delegated conventions and more recently by the entire party membership en masse, makes the leader, once confirmed, accountable to no one. Many people buy memberships in parties solely for the right to vote in a leadership and upon conclusion will let their membership lapse. Accordingly, the constituency that selects the leader disappears almost immediately, making the leader accountable to a no longer existing group.

This phenomenon is so common in Alberta that it has evolved into the concept of the "Rent-a-Tory." With the Progressive Conservative Party enjoying a forty-plus year reign, the dynasty has become a legend: the one-party state. Accordingly, people with little or no connection to PC Alberta will buy $10 memberships in the party, exclusively for the right to vote in the party leadership contests. Given the general non-competitive nature of Alberta general elections, this is often seen as the only meaningful way to participate in who will govern Alberta.

However, the process can easily become hijacked by well-organized special interest groups — groups such as public sector

---

[*] The amended version of the Reform Act increased the requirement to 20 percent.

unions, who do not actually support the PC Party, will nevertheless have a considerable say in crowning its leader, as a result of their members buying thousands of memberships in order to participate.

All of this will change if the Reform Act is passed. Its passage will allow caucuses to elect their chairs and admit or eject caucus members based on the 20/50 percent rules employed to trigger a leadership review. These are currently the exclusive prerogatives of the leader, thus further cementing the leader's control over the caucus.

These changes, if accepted by Parliament, will fundamentally alter the relationship between party leaders and their elected parliamentarians. The leader will become accountable to the caucus; the caucus members will cease to be servants of the leader.

Until 1919, leaders were, in fact, elected by their caucus. I suspect and concede that that day has passed, as party members have a democratic claim to that privilege now. But certainly a leadership review, initiated by caucus and approved by a majority of the caucus, would go a long way to rebalancing democracy by making leaders accountable to their caucus, as opposed to the current system of allowing the leader to essentially choose his or her caucus by maintaining a veto over nominations.

Margaret Thatcher was deposed by her own caucus, and twice in the last four years the Australia Labour Party has rejected a leader (and prime minister) and then rejected the replacement based on the will of the caucus. This is normal; this is parliamentary democracy as it should be, where the leader leads the caucus but does not dominate it. The aforementioned Westminster democracies, which have not fallen prey to creeping presidentialism, are thought to be much more functional by academics and pundits who have studied the comparative systems. Significantly, the mandatory endorsement by a leader of a candidate is absent in those arguably more functional parliamentary democracies.

It is for those reasons that I wholeheartedly endorse the democratic reform initiatives contained in the Reform Act. However, its success in Parliament will require the endorsement of the party leadership of the parties most threatened by its reforms. The rebalancing of the relationship between the leader and the caucus seriously challenges the authority of the prime minister (including future prime ministers). Sadly, I believe, that the current power imbalance ensures a rough ride for the Reform Act.

I fear that a whipped vote in the House, or more likely in a committee, will seal this bill's fate. If that occurs, the irony of the bill's fate should not be lost on Canadians: a legislative initiative designed to empower Members of Parliament will have been defeated by the very powers the bill attempts to reign in.

The conclusion is clear: Power once concentrated is rarely ceded voluntarily.

Libertarians believe that the greatest threat to freedom and rights is the over-concentration of power. A functional democracy requires working checks and balances. Even a benevolent leader requires checks on his or her power. Every system benefits from constructive checks and balances. Sadly, a Canadian prime minister, operating in a majority setting, will find very few constraints on his or her authority.

Some have referred to this concept as the presidentializing of Canadian politics. However, the internal power and influence enjoyed by a Canadian prime minister would be the envy of any U.S. commander-in-chief.

8.

THE PRIME MINISTER'S OFFICE: THE GANG THAT DOESN'T SHOOT STRAIGHT

The object of much of my derision in the days leading up to, and the weeks following, my decision to sever ties with the Conservative caucus is housed in Langevin Block, on Wellington Street in Ottawa.

The Prime Minister's Office is comprised of nearly one hundred members and is divided into several branches. The Policy Branch is comprised of thoughtful and intelligent advisors, tasked with assessing policy proposals and advising the prime minister (and cabinet) on the soundness of policy alternatives. Issues Management and Communications, meanwhile, are staffed by young hyper-partisans, whose task is to assess the political ramifications of any action, proposed or actual, and then spin it in the manner most advantageous to the government.

It is the increasing influence of the Prime Minister's Office generally, and, within the PMO, the relative growth in influence of Issues Management at the expense of Policy, plus Communication Branch's tendency to communicate (spin), frequently with little or no regard for reality, that are the sources of my greatest concern regarding the operation of the executive branch of government. These developments have also been the largest contributing factors to the current government's frequent perception problems with Canadians.

PMO staffers tend to be young, energetic, ambitious, and hyper-partisan. This has not always been the case. Ironically, it was changes regarding the lobbying restrictions for former staffers imposed by the Conservative's signature Accountability Act that led to increasingly inexperienced and younger inhabitants occupying the Langevin Block. Modest pay, by Ottawa standards, for a demanding job that requires long hours attracts a certain type of job applicant. Add to these conditions the lobbying prohibitions that exist post-employment, and the fact that a job with the PMO offers no security of tenure, it is little wonder that the PMO is generally not seen as a suitable place of employment for individuals with mortgages and families to support.

As a result, many PMO staffers are young, very young. It is not uncommon for junior PMO staffers to be hired fresh out of university, many having completed a party internship program during university. The obvious problem is that, although bright and ambitious, many PMO staffers simply lack the job and life experience requisite for the important tasks they are being asked to manage.

As many PMO staffers, especially recent recruits, are in similar situations in life, they migrate to their own subculture. This is natural. Young, single, hyper-partisan politicos working long hours inevitably tend to spend a lot of time together, certainly during extended working hours, but also during limited social engagements. They frequent the same Ottawa watering holes and are more likely to be overheard talking shop than discussing any of the local sports teams.

This description is obviously a generalization and there clearly are exceptions. However, when any group of people who already share significant commonalties and perspectives spend a lot of time together, a tendency evolves for the members of the group to become even more like-minded. These are natural sociological tendencies, and younger people, with less individual experience, are generally more susceptible to become absorbed into existing sub-cultures.

The socialization and indoctrination effects of the PMO sub-culture cannot be overstated. I have witnessed young, seemingly normal and well-adjusted college graduates enter the PMO and, within six months, morph into arrogant, self-absorbed zealots, with an inflated sense of importance and ability.

The result of already like-minded individuals spending almost all of their time together and becoming increasingly more so, is a tendency toward unity of opinion. A tendency for staffers to agree on virtually everything and infrequently disagree with or even challenge the views of each other becomes the product of this work environment. Although most institutions value team players, and there is value in agreement externally, when a group dynamic precludes questioning and challenging each other internally, sycophancy is the inevitable result. Nowhere is this more prevalent than inside the Ottawa Bubble. Although this organizational behaviour model leads to little internal conflict, the inability of it to speak truth to power results in one of the most influential and powerful structures in Ottawa having absolutely no ability to serve as a check on either itself, the prime minister, or the government.

All of this is so significant because of the power of the PMO. Although, formally, the PMO is as an appendage of the prime minister, serving the PM, the Prime Minister's Office has evolved into such a powerful institution in its own right that it is perhaps one of the few institutions in the machinery of government that is actually close enough to the levers of power that it could influence and serve as a check on government authority. As a result, PMO staffers, even relatively junior ones, are revered Ottawa insiders. PMO jobs are highly coveted, and the incumbents are respected, sometimes even feared, by other staffers — even by elected Members of Parliament.

Almost everything that goes on in the Parliamentary Precinct is tightly controlled by the PMO or other executive staffers acting under PMO direction. From the vetting of members' statements, to soliciting backbenchers to ask puffball questions of ministers during Question Period, to the appointment of chairs of parliamentary committees, the PMO's fingerprints are on virtually every file.

PMO staffers can usually get other parliamentary staffers and even parliamentarians to carry out PMO directives, and usually with very little effort. As perquisites such as attending international parliamentary junkets, or political promotions — to parliamentary secretary or cabinet — all require varying degrees of built-up political capital within the Prime Minister's Office, it is seldom that a PMO directive will go ignored. Parliamentarians and staffers alike all curry favour with those within the PMO. This explains why MPs repeat nonsensical talking points, attack Opposition MPs in taxpayer-funded communication products, and, of course, vote as directed by the whip's office, both in the House and also in committee.

I believe that the ability to get staffers and MPs to act as directed, often without even the questioning of the directive, must encourage the growth of a super sense of ego within the young PMO staffers. They have status within the Ottawa Bubble and getting other parts of the Bubble to act as directed must eventually go to their heads. In fact, PMO staffers appear incredulous when their directives are questioned or not obeyed.

I recall one occasion, a junior PMO staffer called my office demanding that a blog post I had written be removed because it was critical of the defence minister's handling of the CF-35 procurement. I made myself deliberately unavailable so the PMO staffer was forced to speak instead to my employee in charge of posting to my website. My staffer stated that "only Mr. Rathgeber has the authority to instruct me to post or remove things from his website."

Incredulous, the PMO Prairie Issues manager responded, "You don't understand; I am calling from the PMO."

To this, my web manager responded, "No, you don't understand, I work for Mr. Rathgeber!"

I am led to believe that PMO staffers are unaccustomed to that level of defiance. Having people generally behave as you like, must eventually go to your head. Invariably, one will develop a swollen ego; perhaps even a sense of near omnipotence.

❖

It should come as no surprise that the PMO was divided over the merits of my private member's bill dealing with public sector salary and expense disclosure. Whereas the Policy wonks saw great merit in forcing disclosure of civil servant salaries, the political advisors saw nothing but landmines. They were concerned (probably correctly) about the number of bad news stories that would be written once it was revealed how much certain senior managers and deputy ministers were earning, not only in salary, but as a result of the more problematic issue of "at risk pay," or bonuses. Currently, although very broad ranges of public servant salaries may be disclosed, the public remains blissfully unaware of the up to 39 percent, or $123,000, which can be earned by a senior deputy minister as a "bonus."

In the end, as it all too frequently does, politics prevailed over policy and loyal foot soldiers were dispatched by PMO to the Access and Privacy Committee to gut PMB C-461. The PMO-directed amendments raised the proposed salary bar to over $444,000, rendering the legislation pointless.

Later, when I chose to leave the Conservative caucus, the PMO jumped on me immediately. On June 5, 2013, mere minutes after I announced on Twitter that I was leaving the caucus, both the current and former directors of PMO Communications (PMO Comms) issued tweets demanding that I resign my seat and run in a by-election to demonstrate that I still maintained the support of Edmonton-St. Albertans. Now, I appreciate that many PMO staffers were not old enough to vote in 2006 and therefore may not remember the David Emerson affair,[1] but I do not believe that defence is available to either director.

Undaunted, even after several media outlets pointed out the hypocrisy in the PMO supporting Emerson's changing of caucuses without seeking re-election but not simply allowing an MP to leave the Conservative caucus to sit alone in the back row, PMO Comms issued talking points parroting the resignation demand of the directors. Armed with these talking points,

Rona Ambrose, the senior minister for Edmonton and area, actually read the lines in the House, apparently forgetting that she was part of the cabinet that welcomed David Emerson in 2006, when he changed parties without a by-election.

Clearly, consistency of message is not something that the PMO always manages to achieve. Indeed, sometimes its efforts to respond to political crises are so unfocused that they seem laughable.

The prize for least effective PMO communication strategy during a crisis would be the so-called "secret fund" used by the PMO to reimburse the public treasury for partisan expenses that are incurred by the prime minister during official government trips. First, according to PMO Comms, the fund did not exist; then it did exist, but was not controlled by the chief of staff. Subsequently, the message was that it existed and was common among all parties and former governments. Finally, the PMO declared that the fund existed and was regulated and monitored by Elections Canada.

Jean-Pierre Kingsley, the former chief electoral officer, subsequently refuted this notion through the media, confirming that Elections Canada has no authority over how party funds are spent outside of an election period. Undoubtedly, most Canadians would take comfort in knowing that taxpayers are reimbursed for partisan activities occurring while the PM is travelling. However, the PMO Communications Branch's inability to get its story straight created suspicion even where none was warranted!

The above PMO Communications gaffes demonstrate pretty obvious strategic errors in the communications strategy of the government. Communication strategy is an imperfect science and even hindsight is frequently imperfect. The mistakes made by the PMO in dealing with the PM's "secret fund" — in terms of communications and in terms of other actions — pale, however, when compared with the mistakes made by the government in response to the Senate Expenses Scandal.

At the same time that the PMO was dealing with the "secret fund" crisis, the prime minister and the PMO were insisting that PM Harper was unaware of the toxic transaction between his then–chief of staff, Nigel Wright, and a sitting senator regarding ineligible housing claims until May 15, 2013. However, PMO Comms issued a statement on May 14, stating that Nigel Wright acted alone in cutting the $90,000 cheque used to reimburse the government for expenses that Senator Mike Duffy had improperly claimed. Not only was the timeline inconsistent, a subsequent RCMP affidavit in support of a search warrant deposes that at least three other PMO staffers were "in the know," that is, that they were aware of Wright's actions.

Are we to believe that none of the other PMO minions questioned this highly unusual transaction? Only in a culture of complete like-mindedness would it be possible for the legal and political liability of the situation to escape multiple minions.

The PMO, however, never admitted that any of the other staff had any knowledge of Wright's dealings. Once the situation became public knowledge, though, PMO Comms sprang into action, issuing laughable talking points: Mr. Wright was a patriot, so concerned about taxpayers that he dug into his own resources to ensure that taxpayers were not left subsidizing ineligible expense claims. Four days later, Wright was unemployed and the object of immediate vilification by the PMO. Each version of the events described by the PMO became less credible than the one that preceded it!

The decision by the prime minister's chief of staff to "gift" $90,000 to a sitting senator in order to mitigate a damaging scandal takes lack of judgment to new and dangerous heights (or lows)! The action was the product of an obvious legal and ethical lapses of judgment, and was the subject of an RCMP investigation to determine if a fraud was committed against the government, or if influence was peddled and/or purchased.

The Wright/Duffy affair is a disturbing example of a dangerous lack of separation between the executive and legislative branches of the Canadian government. Both houses of Parliament exist to hold government to account. How likely is it, however, that a senator is going to seriously vet government legislation when that senator is indebted financially to the executive branch's top political aide?

It is consistent with standard operating procedure that the PMO was driving the bus on this debacle, that the PMO persuaded Senator Duffy to participate in this unusual scheme to "claim" to be paying money back in an attempt to mitigate the consequences of the impending audit into the senator's expenses. I cannot defend the actions of Senator Duffy but do believe that he went along the scheme in order to protect his Senate seat after questions about his residency were held over him.

In dribs and drabs, it is becoming apparent that the PMO attempted to make a scandal involving one of its more high-profile appointments go away in order to spare itself any embarrassment. Laws were allegedly broken; regardless of whether they were or not, however, the entire episode is a dramatic display of why Canadian democracy is unbalanced. Under a system of responsible government, the executive is supposed to be accountable to the legislature. In reality, the legislative branch is deferential to, and even fearful of, the executive — especially the Prime Minister's Office.

The consequences of an omnipotent PMO are obvious. They include a belief amongst the PMO chieftains that the rules don't apply to them, that anything can be "fixed," including a senator's ineligible housing expenses. The frightening thing is that in the case of the senators involved in the Senate Expenses Scandal they almost got away with it. Neither Parliament nor the public know what other potential scandals the PMO has successfully "fixed."

It is not difficult to understand why PMO fixers believe they can solve any crisis. Any unelected institution that can get elected parliamentarians, and therefore parliamentary institutions, to move as directed will inevitably believe there are no moving parts beyond their reach.

The Prime Minister's Office has far too much power. Its staffers lack the experience and maturity required to handle the power they have been given. Given the loss of credibility and prestige that the PMO is suffering as a result of the Wright/Duffy debacle, now is a critical time for the public, the media, and especially Parliament to scale back the influence of the Prime Minister's Office.

POLITICAL PARTIES: POWER IS AN END IN ITSELF

Contrary to anything that you have read in this book, I am not, in fact, opposed to political parties. I have belonged to several over the years, both provincial and federal. I have served on boards of directors for local riding associations and attended countless conventions and annual general meetings.

I believe that political parties do serve an important function in our democratic process. The term "political party" is not to be found anywhere in the Canadian Constitution. Technically, they are not part of the machinery of government, and formally and constitutionally they are not institutions whose role it is to hold government to account. However, given the political party's ever-present and real role in the Canadian polity, they merit a brief examination and discussion in a treatise on broken democracy.

Political parties play a critical role in the electoral process; in fact, they are indispensable. If their influence was limited to the electoral process, they would be largely unassailable. However, it is their constant creep into the appointment and policy processes that is cause for concern amongst defenders of accountable and responsible government.

Sadly, most voters are largely disengaged from the political process and are largely ignorant of the choices that are being presented to them during elections. If every Canadian citizen were a politico and spent hundreds of hours researching, dissecting, and comparing policy alternatives, there would be less need for political parties to distill the issues for them.

That is not the case, however. So, the political party does the casual political observer a valuable service by distilling a plethora of policy choices into broad menus that allow the voter to pick one from usually four realistic choices.

Although fewer Canadians are voting based on tradition, on how their grandfather and father voted, they still largely identify with one party or another. Generally, voters will informally identify themselves as being progressive or conservative, and it is usually by appealing to those broad parameters that political parties will attempt to sway the voter to their particular brands.

For candidates, political parties provide the advantage of being incredible fundraising machines, able to assist with mass marketing campaigns and call centres, and, by the means of arrangements made with the tax authorities, able to offer generous tax credits to contributors. Moreover, political parties offer candidates immeasurable economies of scale when it comes to persuading and identifying voters and getting them to the polls on election day.

Lawn signs are much more affordable when purchased in bulk, with consistent branding, where the only variable is the name of the candidate. As a candidate in an urban/metro riding, I found it much more cost effective to share a large advertisement in a metro daily paper with fellow party candidates than would have been the case for me, even if each of us had taken out a much smaller ad and run it less frequently.

Finally, political parties are able to purchase the software necessary to track voter support and ensure that identified voters are assisted, if necessary, to make it to the polling station on election day.

What is common among all of the identified, above listed, advantages of political parties is that they all involve some aspect of the electoral process. I readily admit that political parties are invaluable in identifying voters, raising money, purchasing mass media, and distilling and simplifying issues for the voter.

That value can be seen in the negative in municipal elections, where political parties do not play a significant role. Although voter turnout is disappointing in all electoral contests, it is especially dismal during municipal elections. Sadly, it is not uncommon for as few as one third of eligible voters to cast ballots for mayors, councillors, and county reeves. At least part of the explanation for this truly dismal level of voter participation is the lack of party organization at the municipal level. With no political parties to distill multiple and complicated issues to three or four credible choices, disengaged voters may not take the time to assess those issues on their own. Additionally, there is generally no "machine" at the municipal level, where political parties are either entirely absent or less organized than at the provincial or federal levels, to get out the vote or purchase economical large scale advertising.

Again, a strong case for the value of political parties for both political aspirants and voter participation can fairly easily be made.

❖

What is the situation after elections and between them? Do political parties contribute positively or negatively to holding government to account? Unfortunately, it is increasingly becoming the latter as political parties' preoccupation with success at the next electoral contest precludes any meaningful role in holding party or government to account between election cycles.

At both the federal and provincial levels, political parties exist both nationally (or provincially) and at the local level, continuously and between elections. Political parties are active fifty-two weeks a year, mailing information to party members and encouraging them to donate to the cause. The advent of e-mail and other social media have made this process more timely and inexpensive.

Well-organized parties will have local riding associations, or electoral district associations (EDAs), made of the members of the party who live in that geographic riding or electoral district. The riding association will have an annual general meeting (AGM), where an executive will be duly elected. They will hold monthly meetings and at least one annual fundraiser to build up a war chest for the next election. At the appropriate time, they will strike a nomination committee to recruit and vet appropriate candidates and then hold a contest, called a nomination, where the riding association will choose their candidate for the next election.

The nomination process is a bizarre and often divisive period, where partisans of the same colour and usually from the same riding are pitted against one another. In a "good" nomination, the vote will result in no more than disappointment and hard feelings from the losing side. Less successful nominations will produce mass resignations, destroyed friendships, and litigation as collateral damage.

There are no tactics too nasty, mean-spirited, or illegal to be employed during party nominations. A non-exhaustive list of attempts to gain advantage during the nomination process include: the bussing in of non-constituents with fake address identification; the paying of voters for support (including supplying the fee required to purchase a party membership); and juvenile attempts at voter suppression, such as occupying all available parking spots to make it more difficult for non-supporters to access the nomination hall.

In 2007, during my nomination for the Conservative Party of Canada, my main opposition used a false endorsement from the national campaign chairman on his website, and invented an entire online news magazine (from Washington State of all places) that covered the Edmonton-St. Albert Nomination, almost exclusively, replete with defamatory articles about my campaign, me, and my family, and glowing op-ed pieces on their favoured candidate.

But what is it all for? The nomination is little more than a popularity contest. The winner will be chosen based on which candidate, and his or her team, can sell the most memberships and thereafter get the most purchasers of those memberships out to the voting hall. Qualifications and knowledge of pertinent issues are secondary considerations. The ability to sell $10 party memberships is what qualifies one to be the party's flag bearer.

This bizarre method of choosing an electoral candidate serves only the party's interest. More memberships translate into more money in the bank for the party and more names in the supporter database. The quality of the candidate who sold the memberships is secondary, as he or she will likely become mere window dressing for the party.

In fact, I have come to conclude that political parties are actually not interested in recruiting bright and articulate candidates. Smart people tend to be critical thinkers. Critical thinking produces informed discussion, which is contrary to the political apparatus's goal of having a carefully crafted message that is delivered by torch bearers who stay on script and unequivocally support the party and the party leader.

If the political apparatus has an incentive to recruit a candidate for qualities other than membership sales ability, it is less likely to be policy competence than representation of a certain demographic. Women, especially telegenic ones, and visible minorities are frequently sought-after political assets.

To the extent that the party has any interest in a nomination outcome, it is only the candidate's ability to acquire votes that interests the party brass. Sadly, a grasp of issues and intelligence are less valuable in the electoral calculation than is the candidate's mastery of electoral consumerism (formerly known as retail politics). In the eyes of the party, the ability to sell memberships and get purchasers out to the nomination meeting represents an ability to connect with the voter. Extra points are given to representatives of underrepresented demographic groups. Free-thinking policy analysts are considered to be likely more trouble than they are worth. They will be less complacent, less placating, and more likely to morph into mavericks — possibly even liberated Independents!

Politicos will tell you that the candidate is little more than a hood ornament on the electoral machine, a commonplace that confirms my theories concerning the worthlessness of the party nomination process and irrelevance of who emerges successfully. Occasionally, however, something goes awry, and a local riding association elects a candidate who isn't deemed likely to play the role of puppet that the party's masters demand of local candidates. When that happens, when the national party disapproves, for whatever reason, of the candidate chosen, or of any other activity of a local riding association, the errant riding association experiences just how democratic the entire process can be. When it smells too much democracy or any other matter that it will have difficulty controlling, the national council will actually intervene and literally take over a riding association.

This occurred, most recently, following the annual general meeting of the Calgary West Electoral District Association (CPC). Opponents of the incumbent MP, Rob Anders, flooded the AGM and were able to gain control of the board of directors. The national council, however, promptly disallowed the elections, seized the riding association's bank accounts and membership lists, and then appointed a new and more acceptable board of directors.[1]

All of these extraordinary measures are permissible under "appropriate circumstances" in the Conservative Party constitution. When it occurs, however, traditional, reform-minded members of the party grieve the complete trampling and destruction of grassroots democracy.

The other big process of the political party is the annual or biannual general meeting and policy conference. This allows, at least in theory, grassroots members and local riding associations to submit, debate, and vote on policy resolutions, which in theory would become part of the party's policy handbook.

In reality, this process is so tightly controlled that it barely qualifies as a process. At the end of the day, its only value is to give the grassroots members, and convention delegates, the illusionary feeling that they are part of the process and that their policy ideas are valued. In practice, the vetting process is controlled and managed to ensure that no controversial or potentially embarrassing policy resolution ever makes it onto the floor of the convention.

The party's masters know that even policy resolutions with little chance of passing will be picked up and reported by the mainstream media; they are aware that anything discussed on the convention floor will be commented upon by opposition parties in their insatiable need to embarrass the party in question in an attempt to make their own party look moderate by comparison. Given the advent of social and micromedia, these concerns are all the more important to the party operatives. Why, they think, should the party risk alienating any voter group or demographic when they can simply design a system of internal checks to guarantee that no potentially problematic resolutions make it onto the convention floor for a vote? A better solution is to vet them away before the convention commences.

The Conservative Party of Canada has a sophisticated system that commences almost a year before the general policy convention. Local electoral district associations are invited to submit policy resolutions. The first step in this process involves the striking of a policy committee within the local EDA. After the committee designs and then vets potential ideas, the resolutions will be presented to the entire EDA board for approval.

If a resolution (policy idea) has the approval of the local EDA, it will then be submitted to, and further vetted by, a policy congress, or regional party vetting mechanism. Presumably, anything too hot or controversial will be caught by this two-step congress.

At the policy congress, breakout sessions divide policy resolutions into broad policy categories. Show-of-hands support will take "successful" resolutions to a secondary plenary vote of the entire congress. All of this occurs in camera, away from the prying eyes of the media.

Policy resolutions supported by the regional congresses will then be submitted to the policy committee of the national council to assure compliance with the party constitution and general policy framework. Decisions of the national council are final; this provides a veto over any proposed policy the powers-that-be do not support or which they find potentially politically problematic.

Then, at the actual general meeting and policy convention, those resolutions that have survived thus far are again subject to the same two-step vetting process employed at the regional congresses. Breakout sessions organized by broad policy category (environment, justice, the economy, et cetera) again vet resolutions behind closed doors. Then, on the final day of the convention, the media is invited into the plenary session, where a final vote by all delegates determines which surviving policy resolutions will make it into the party's policy handbook.

However, as onerous as this vetting process is, it is deemed inadequate for guaranteeing that only "approved" policy resolutions make it to the final vote. So, another way of vetting resolutions is added to the process. Time limitations are perhaps the most arbitrary system to vet away undesirable policy suggestions. There is only so much time to debate and vote on all of the resolutions. As a result, resolutions are ranked according to level of support. Those with overwhelming support in the breakout meetings are ranked ahead of those with smaller majority support. This decision is entirely subjective, though, as most votes are determined only by a show of hands, with no record kept of the results. On top of that, the national council chooses the chairs of each and every policy session, so the people deciding the results of the votes are all appointees of the national council. With everything set up by the national council, the party's ability to sidestep both problematic resolutions and democracy is complete.

Surviving the above process is almost impossible unless the resolution is supported by the party establishment, in which case approval is virtually guaranteed. If a resolution that lacks support by the party leaders does manage to win support, there is still a way to ensure that it has no effect. Although policies approved by this arduous vetting process will make it into the party's policy handbook, they are not binding on the party or on the government. The fact that approved resolutions are not binding confirms that the entire process is for show, to give party loyalists a false sense of efficacy in their party's policy development.

❖

Not only has the democratic character of political parties been in decline lately, as seen by the suppression of alternative viewpoints at the riding level and at party AGMs, recently, parties have also been involved in voter suppression techniques that arguably negate the effect that they might otherwise have on voter participation.

The most explicit example of this occurred in the 2011 federal election. In what became known as the Robocall scandal, it is alleged that automatic dialers were used to call non-supporters of the Conservative Party in Guelph, Ontario, to advise them, erroneously, that their polling station had been changed and direct them to a non-existent polling station.

More subtle attempts at voter suppression exist, including character assassination of alternative candidates and party leaders, and negative advertising generally. The goal of these negative marketing techniques is not to convince a voter (inclined to support the other candidate or leader) to change his vote, but simply to raise enough suspicion of the voter's likely choice, that he will end up not voting at all.

Sadly, these electoral techniques are often successful. They demonstrate the "win at all costs" philosophy of political parties. Rules are bent, if not broken, and the ends will justify the means in this holy war between one party and the forces of political evil, such as the politico sees them.

The problem is that elections are not merely a game, where the only relevant result is winning or losing. Elections are the means we employ to determine who will govern us. The stakes are much higher and important than mere victory or defeat.

However, hyper-partisans, devoid of ideology or principle, see electoral victory as the only relevant endgame. To a growing class of young political operatives, winning is a critical end in itself, rather than a mere means to a more important end: choosing a responsible and accountable government. That explains why such political zealots are increasingly attracted to, and employed by, political (electoral) operations, rather than within the policy development machinery of government.

The problems associated with political parties being so influential and contributing to a broken democracy are exacerbated by how opaquely they operate.

Members of the Conservative Party of Canada were shocked and outraged to discover that they, through the Conservative Canada Fund, had contributed over $13,000 to cover embattled Senator Mike Duffy's legal expenses. Worse, they would have never found out about this misuse of their financial donations had the embattled senator kept his mouth shut concerning the unusual, and possibly illegal, transactions, surrounding his ineligible expense claims.

The fund is managed by a director, appointed by the leader; in the case of the Conservatives, that is the prime minister. Only the director can determine how the fund is allocated. Party members and donors have absolutely no say in how the fund is used, and they cannot replace the leader's chosen financial director.

Moreover, political parties are not subject to access to information legislation, nor do they have any public disclosure responsibilities. Ironically, C-377,[2] a private member's bill supported by the Conservative caucus and government, sought to force trade unions to disclose essentially all of their financial information on a publically accessible website. The tenuous argument to support this proposition was that the tax deductibility of union dues created a public interest, since the union dues are forgone public dollars.

As tenuous as this logic is, it was also being surgically applied. Political parties operate, not on the basis of tax-deductible dues, but on the basis of the much more generous tax-credited donations. So generous are political tax credits that the real cost to the donor of a $100 donation to a party or candidate is a mere $25.

Yet I neither see nor expect to see a comparable effort to subject political parties to any financial disclosure requirements, much less the invasive ones that were proposed for trade unions. When it comes to transparency, the words "not in my backyard" continue to ring loud inside the Ottawa Bubble.

For all of the aforementioned reasons, I believe that the only time when there is a legitimate role for political parties to play is during the election cycle. Given their opaqueness and their growing influence between election periods, they are enablers and contributors to the growing democratic deficit currently plaguing Canada.

10.

THE BUREAUCRACY:
INFORMATION IS POWER

In any examination of the various institutions of government and how each is failing Canadians in holding their government to account it is, of course, necessary to consider the permanent government. What role does the public service play in holding government to account?

It is perhaps counterintuitive that the government bureaucracy, the permanent government, which exists to serve, advise, and carry out the directives of the political government (the cabinet), is part of the machinery designed to provide a check on government power. In a perfect world, the public service would serve the public, and the elected heads of government and the permanent bureaucracy would always be in sync.

However, we do not live in a perfect world. Governments do things they should not. And for the bureaucracy, there are the realities of patronage, partisan loyalties, and differences of ideological perspective and opinion, all of which have accelerated, retarded, or even terminated the careers of many public servants.

It is within this context of potential conflict that a public servant can, and occasionally does, serve as a functional check on government. This can occur when the public servant serves in the role of a watchdog, or it can happen when an employee believes that the government is acting improperly and the public servant goes public with his or her concerns. However, as this chapter will examine, deliberate attempts to politicize and then discredit watchdogs such as the parliamentary budget officer and inadequate whistle-blower protection for federal public servants have seriously compromised the ability of the public service to hold government to account.

❖

The current federal government sees the public service as too large, too expensive, and too resistant to change. As a result, the current political masters have been deliberately attempting to diminish and dispirit the public service. In the Ottawa Bubble, where absolute loyalty and the unquestioning following of directives has rapidly become the norm, toadying is certainly preferred to speaking truth to power.

Some brave and notable exceptions do occasionally present themselves. Parliamentary Budget Officer Kevin Page was a constant irritant to the cabinet and the Prime Minister's Office every time he released a report questioning their budget numbers and projections. Similarly, diplomat Richard Colvin angered the government when he went public with serious allegations regarding Canadian treatment of Afghan detainees.[1]

From time to time, a whistle-blower will come forward with the courage to correct a lie or shine light on government mismanagement or bureaucratic bungling. Employment Insurance Investigator Sylvie Therrien disclosed that she was forced to maintain quotas and that EI claimants were harassed or improperly penalized so that those quotas might be achieved. Each investigator was required to claim back $485,000 or more in benefits per annum. Investigators, she claimed publically, were encouraged to interpret disputed facts in such a way that would deny benefits. Therrien was suspended without pay and eventually fired for leaking confidential documents.[2]

The government claims that the $485,000 was a target and not a quota. However, if bonuses are conditional upon meeting one's target, I am not sure that there is an appreciable difference.

In 2013, the Clerk of the Privy Council Office released his plan to renew and reinvigorate the federal public service.[3] It was largely fluff, addressing citizen engagement and smart use of new technologies. But nothing in the plan addresses the degree of independence that the federal bureaucracy once enjoyed.

For a government that was elected in 2006 on a promise of accountability and open government, it does everything in its power to ensure opacity. It must be said that governments of all stripes have been tightening control over communications within and by the public service for two decades, but the level of control has been accelerated by the current messaging-obsessed government.

As well, a shift in government priorities has been de-emphasizing scientific knowledge in favour of commercial-based research directed toward exploiting natural resources, especially in the northern Arctic. Scientists, as a result, have entered the unfamiliar world of political advocacy, protesting crippling cuts to their research projects and a changed emphasis on economic development over acquired knowledge.

The Professional Institute of the Public Service of Canada surveyed four thousand of its members; 24 percent of respondents claimed that they had been asked to exclude or alter technical information in government documents for non-scientific reasons, and 37 percent reported that they had been prevented from responding to media requests regarding topics within their expertise.[4]

Most notably, half of the four thousand respondents claimed that they were aware of cases where either the health or safety of Canadians or environmental sustainability had been compromised because of political interference with their scientific research. Nearly three-quarters believed that their ability to develop policy, law, and programs based on scientific evidence had been compromised by political interference.

While many scientists deny being directly prevented from speaking to the public or the media about their research, they claim a "climate of fear" which accomplishes the same result. The PIPSC survey supports longstanding fears of a developing pattern of interference in the ability of government scientists to communicate to the public their science and their findings "without being controlled."

As a result, communications specialists within government began to insist on unity of messaging and that messaging became political not fact-based. The government was becoming more discriminate in what it wanted its researchers to tell them. Science that supported industry and commerce was welcome; that which raised inconvenient truths regarding climate change, diminishing habitats, or damaged ecosystems was less well received.

However, science represents knowledge. What the decision maker does with that knowledge is a matter of assessing priority options. That is a political decision. The wise decision-maker does not deny herself the benefit of research and alternative findings to assist in the choosing of the best policy alternative.

You cannot run a democracy or make decisions without facts, even, or perhaps especially, those facts that do not fit neatly with your predetermined policy priorities. Both the public and the decision-makers must be informed in order to weigh costs versus benefits.

As an Alberta MP, I promote responsible oil sands development. But I want accurate information regarding the environmental consequences so that I can make informed decisions regarding the pace of oil sand development. Similarly, those who would be against pipeline projects should receive accurate research and projections regarding economic benefits forgone before making a final decision. Policy should not drive science; science should contribute to an informed policy debate.

Muzzling or defunding scientific research that does not support a particular political agenda leads inexorably to bad decision making and an uninformed public. It is an unaccountable government that politicizes science, muzzling it or massaging results to drive political spin.

❖

Civil servants are allowed by law to alert the public directly if they are aware of serious government malfeasance, but only if there is insufficient time to exhaust all internal avenues. The government believes that public servants have many internal avenues to air those grievances. Public servants believe that the time-consuming internal processes are designed deliberately to prevent whistle-blowing. I believe that for public servants to serve as an effective check on government authority, they must, under the appropriate circumstances, go public with their observations of corruption, malfeasance, and incompetence.

For decades, whistle-blowers have faced sufficient reprisal inside the workplace to serve as a deterrent against them going public. Initial reprisals can and do include poor performance reviews, reassignment to less meaningful work, smear campaigns by senior management, being shunned by colleagues, blatant warnings to cease and desist, and reassignment to a less sought after location or office.

Public servants who suffered a crisis of conscience faced even more daunting consequences if they decided to go public with their concerns. Their government employer, with unlimited resources and legions of lawyers and private investigators, could make life for the whistle-blower very unpleasant. The whistle-blower would invariably get a bad reputation and likely become unemployable.

Clearly, if there is a public interest in whistle-blowing, whistle-blowers require protection. I believe that there is great public interest in exposing the truth. Corruption is like a cancer that threatens the entire roots of our democracy. Recent events in the Senate of Canada reinforce the public interest in employees "snitching" on their bosses if there have been misappropriations, abusing of expense accounts, or cases of sexual or other harassment in the workplace.

Malfeasance or incompetence can lead to a massive waste of public resources, flawed and abandoned projects, and compromised public health and safety, defense, energy, and environmental policies. With a federal government spending $500 million every day, the cost of government mismanagement is potentially immense.

Sunlight is always the best disinfectant, and, accordingly, public disclosure of corruption and malfeasance leads to better accountability of government at all levels. As a result, whistle-blower protection is required to protect those courageous enough to risk their careers to shine the light on government wrongdoing.

The requirement, however, is for strong and effective legislation that provides and protects public servants' right to speak out, ensures that any allegations they raise are investigated and taken seriously, and makes illegal the harsh retaliation against public servants who speak out that is such an effective deterrent to whistle-blowing.

It is for these reasons that advocates for effective whistle-blowing protection are so disappointed and frustrated by Canada's response. Under Canada's so-called whistle-blower protection law,[5] a grievance is considered a "comprehensive remedy" for employees threatened by reprisal, a fact that denies them legal recourse against their superiors, who are frequently in charge of managing the grievance process!

Moreover, large segments of the public service, including the Canadian Forces, CSIS, and for, practical purposes, the RCMP, are excluded from the act. RCMP members must first exhaust internal complaints procedures before even filing a complaint with the integrity commissioner. However, as the ongoing Edward Snowden/National Security Advisor imbroglio continues to unravel, it is becoming clearer that it is within national security agencies that some of the greatest potential for malfeasance exists and therefore it is within those agencies that the requirement for effective whistle-blower protection is the greatest.

With much fanfare and at a cost of $8 million per year, a whistle-blowing protection process was introduced in Canada as part of the 2006 Accountability Act. However, the act, by insisting on exhausting internal grievance processes before going public, has the effect of putting whistle-blowers in an even more precarious position than existed previously. They have lost their common law right to sue their employer; instead, they have been granted the opportunity to make use of a secretive, internal administrative grievance procedure, which, though it may not have been designed specifically to do so, has had the effect of further keeping damaging allegations hidden from the public.

The public service integrity commissioner has broad discretion to refrain from investigating something if it is deemed to not be "in the public interest," or for any other "valid reason." These are vague exemptions, granting the commissioner the discretion to do nothing in a wide variety of cases. Even when the commissioner chooses to investigate, however, the commissioner has no order-making power, and no power to sanction harassment or to take any corrective actions. The integrity commissioner is limited to reporting the wrongdoing to the relevant department head and then to Parliament.

If, in the end, a whistle-blowing case is settled by the government, the government can insist on a gag order — further, and permanently, preventing the whistle-blower from going to the media.

Canada's first integrity commissioner found exactly zero cases of reprisal, and Christianne Ouimet's successor has done only marginally better. Obviously, some changes in the rules regarding the whistle-blowing process are required if it is to become more effective; however, the legally mandated five-year review of the legislation is over two years past due. The delay has the effect of further denying the opportunity to implement much-needed reforms to the fatally flawed legislation.

Apart from the federal government, only six out of ten Canadian provinces have any whistle-blower protection, and Alberta's recent attempt provides even less protection than Canada's. Amazingly, the legislation there allows the commissioner to exempt from the act "any person, class of persons, public entity, information, record or thing."[6] The law contains no remedies or order-making power and there is no mechanism to challenge the commissioner's decisions, which can remain secret forever.

It would appear that both the federal and the Alberta governments have deliberately designed whistle-blower protection systems that foster even more opacity, despite the supposed aim of providing transparency and accountability. The systems operate inside a bubble, with impenetrable secrecy, denying legal remedies to those who would challenge them and seemingly serving the interests of their respective governments rather than those of the whistle-blower.

As other jurisdictions, such as the United States and United Kingdom have discovered, the single best method of detecting institutional wrongdoing is to listen to employees. The Association of Certified Fraud Examiners confirms that the best source for exposing fraud is tips from employees and anonymous sources (43 percent).[7] It is critical to protect whistle-blowers, as they are often the last line of defence when all other checks and balances within the system have failed.

❖

Given the weakness of Canada's whistle-blower protection laws, the limitations on the bureaucracy's ability to hold government to account due to their inherently conflicted position as they are part of the government, and Parliament's declining ability to hold governments to account, it is increasingly falling on the officers of Parliament to provide an oversight role. Some, such as the Office of the Auditor General, have proved effective at providing government oversight, but the AG is limited to disclosing financial mismanagement after it has occurred. Others could provide a meaningful check on government, such as the access to information commissioner, but toothless enabling legislation, including a lack of order-making power, reduces that role to one of advisor only.

The creation of the Office of the Parliamentary Budget Officer was announced with great fanfare as part of the 2006 Accountability Act. The great expectations were soon replaced by frustrated disappointment, however. The PBO, conceptually, provides independent analysis to Parliament on the state of the nation's finances, the government's estimates, and trends in the economy, and, upon request, it also supplies the estimated financial cost of any program or proposal.

True fiscal conservatives, like me, were ecstatic when the creation of the PBO was announced. Since Parliament had surrendered examination of the increasingly complex expenditure plans of government by 1972, and since the Office of the Comptroller General had been emasculated by the same time, there had been a profound lack of analysis of government budgeting. Finally, it seemed, there would be independent financial oversight of government budgets and spending.

Partisan Conservatives, however, were nervous. What if the PBO issued reports critical of the government? they worried. What if the office turned out to be a watchdog rather than a lap dog?

Partisan concerns were soon verified; the PBO proceeded to release reports that questioned or criticized government spending or budgeting. Every time he did so, however, the government was dismissive. Undeterred, the first parliamentary budget officer continued to release critical reports. In response, the government that created the PBO began to attack Mr. Page personally, accusing him of having a partisan (Opposition) agenda.

The last allegation, ironically, had a ring of truth to it. Because government backbenchers believe their role is to cheerlead for the government rather than ask tough (or any) questions of it, it was only the Opposition that was requesting PBO reports and assessments. But, this situation was entirely due to government backbenchers not understanding their role; Mr. Page understood his role perfectly.

The relationship between the government and the PBO deteriorated significantly in the spring of 2011 when the PBO published a peer-reviewed analysis concluding that the cost of the government's F-35 procurement was $29.3 billion, over three times higher than the Department of National Defence's $9 billion public estimate.[8] A year later, the auditor general similarly concluded that DND had grossly underestimated the cost of the Joint Strike Fighter program.

By 2012, the government was in full attack mode, working overtime to undermine the parliamentary budget officer. The finance minister and Treasury Board president attacked Kevin

Page's credibility. A growing number of departments actually refused to disclose information to the PBO regarding such matters as the cost and projected savings of proposed budget cuts, claiming them as being outside of the PBO's mandate. This was an amazing development, given that the PBO is statutorily entitled to the information. The Parliament of Canada Act states that the PBO is "entitled by request made to the deputy head of a department … free and timely access to *any* [my italics] financial or economic data in the possession of the department that are required for the performance of his or her mandate."[9]

The parliamentary budget officer actually had to take the government to Federal Court and was reduced to filing access to information requests in a feeble attempt to get the documents required to do its job. It is both astonishing and unacceptable that a budget watchdog has been put in the penalty box for doing its job! The extreme irony is that if the Conservatives were still the Opposition they would continue to believe in the value of the office, its reports, and its analyses.

With the departure of Mr. Page, it became clear that the government's loathing of the PBO was not the product of a personal dislike of him. His interim replacement, Sonia L'Heureux, issued a statement in July of 2013 alleging that many government departments were still refusing to provide her office with requisite details related to spending cuts in the Economic Action Plan 2012.[10] Since then, the permanent replacement, Jean-Denis Frechette, has confirmed that the government still refuses to fully comply with almost half of the budget watchdog's requests for information and data. This has impeded the PBO in analyzing 40 percent of government programs.[11] This is an untenable situation. The current government created the

Parliamentary Budget Office; the same government now stonewalls its requests for information.

Government budgets are complex, voluminous documents. Parliamentarians simply do not have enough time and resources to adequately assess them. In 2011, the government was held in contempt of Parliament for refusing to provide Parliament with estimates for the F-35 procurement, corporate tax cuts, various crime bills, and hosting costs for the G20 Summit.

Parliament's primary role, since its inception in England in 1236, has been to scrutinize and then approve government spending. With estimates deemed to be approved by June 23, it hasn't done the latter since 1972. With a government refusing to provide Parliament and its officers the required data, it can no longer even provide scrutiny. The government refuses to allow itself to be held to account and Parliament cannot seem to do anything about it. Unless this situation changes, it must be concluded that we no longer have responsible government in Canada.

11. _174

WITHHOLDING THE POWER: CANADA'S BROKEN ACCESS TO INFORMATION LAWS

As with Parliament, access to information regimes have an important role in holding government to account. Properly functioning access laws allow citizens, the media, and academics access to information about what their government is up to. Proper access laws lead to trust between citizens and the state; improperly functioning access laws lead to suspicion, mistrust, and, ultimately, to less government accountability.

Canada was once the poster child country for access to information legislation. When Canada passed its first access act in 1983, it was considered a benchmark that other Western democracies would replicate and model their own regimes after. But thirty years later, the experiment is beginning to fail us. New electronic and cyber technologies have evolved; Canada's access laws have not.

In 1983, Canada was one of the first Western democracies, and the first Westminster system of government, to pass and proclaim access to information legislation. As with other pioneering jurisdictions, our access regime was premised on the principle that openness and transparency would make government more accountable and therefore responsive.

The original Access to Information Act[1]:

- Confirmed the right of citizens to access government information;
- Established a presumption in favour of disclosure;
- Defined clear limitations and exceptions to disclosure;
- Required government institutions to process requests in a timely manner;
- And provided a right of appeal to citizens who believe they have been wrongfully denied information.

The act was ahead of its time, and its drafters were rightfully proud. The act has been called an essential component of a vibrant democracy, because nothing is more fundamental to a democracy than an informed public.

About the same time, Canada also received a Charter of Rights and Freedoms. Although a right to know is not a Charter-protected right, a right of access to information is inextricably linked to freedom of thought, freedom of speech, and certainly freedom for the media. Access to information allows Canadians to more fully participate in the democratic process and to hold their governments to account. The right to information promotes accountability and keeps government honest.

The 1983 Access to Information Act had, however, both its limitations and its detractors. It had many exemptions — it was specifically crafted so that it did not apply to Parliament, the Prime Minister's Office, or, originally, Crown corporations. It required those seeking access to pay fees, lacked a public-interest test for determining the legitimacy of most exemptions, and denied the information commissioner order-making authority.

Imperfections aside, it was cutting edge for 1983. It was assumed that successive governments would build on the original access foundations. Yet, in the thirty years since its implementation, only marginal and piecemeal changes have been made to federal access laws. The current government, through its signature Accountability Act, increased the number of institutions to which the regime applied, most notably Crown corporations. However, the same amendments added some specific and most unhelpful institutional exemptions and exclusions.

Every annual report of every information commissioner calls for a comprehensive overview of the entire regime to bring the act into the twenty-first century. Each government-in-waiting promises to overhaul the federal Access to Information Act and bring in open and transparent government. Once they become government, however, they suddenly have more pressing matters to deal with and access to information ceases to be a priority.

It has become readily apparent that Canada's federal government is no longer an international leader in access to government information law. Canada was recently ranked fifty-fifth out of ninety-three countries in regards to open and transparent government.[2] According to the Centre for Law and Democracy, Canada, once top tier, is no longer in the top fiftieth percentile when it comes to transparent government. Even within Canada, the federal government is no longer a leader. It has fallen behind most of the provinces and territories in defining a citizen's right to know.

Respective information commissioners have recognized that the access regime is outdated. In 2005, Commissioner John Reid, at the request of the Parliamentary Committee on Access to Information, Privacy, and Ethics, tabled a draft reform bill called the Open Government Act. It was a complete rewrite of the Access to Information Act, and included an update of its provisions and a new name. Commissioner Reid's proposals would have increased number of institutions to which the act was applicable, reduced the scope of limitations restricting its utility, and expanded the commissioner's oversight authority.[3]

In 2006, the newly elected Conservative government rode into Ottawa promising a complete overhaul of federal access laws. Moreover, it undertook to implement the recommendations of former Commissioner Reid. Instead, the government replaced Reid as commissioner and shelved his report. Of the recommendations, only expanding the scope of the legislation to include Crown corporations made its way into the 2006 Accountability Act, notwithstanding the fact that the Access Committee recommended that the government consider Commissioner Reid's Open Government Act.[4]

Three years later, Commissioner Robert Marleau made twelve recommendations that he believed were urgently required to modernize Canada's access laws and catch up to other international benchmarks. Marleau's proposals covered such issues as timeliness, order-making power for the commissioner, compliance, public education, and the coverage of the act, which would be expanded to include the institutions of Parliament, cabinet confidences, and even the courts. In a June 2009 report to Parliament,[5] the Standing Committee on Access agreed with all of Marleau's recommendations. Despite that, however, the entire report has been shelved.

The current information commissioner, Suzanne Legault, has joined the speaking circuit and in the media has referred to the system as "busting." She referred to the legislation as "tired, outdated and constricted by too many limitations."[6] According to the commissioner, there are two basic problems with the 1983 Access to Information Act. The first is the fact that is has not been updated to deal with the advent of electronic data; the second is the increase in size and complexity of government and the centralization of decision making.

Electronic files simply did not exist when the regime was created in 1983. Back then, documents were paper-based and stored in filing cabinets. Today, most government information is in electronic or digital format. That creates challenges for tracking information — it is often very difficult to find records for material that is transmitted on smartphones or via texting, where no paper trail is established. Such information does not generally go through a departmental server, and therefore it is difficult to trace.

There is a growing body of evidence which suggests that government bureaucrats, and especially political staff, are increasingly conducting their business verbally, without retaining notes; or, alternatively, they are exchanging correspondence through private email addresses that are not part of government and/or employing digital devices that leave no trace. Although there are penalties for destroying documents, there is no positive obligation to create documents.

Regarding the changes that have occurred in government organization, Legault states that increase in the size of government has resulted in a 50 percent increase in her office's workload. Her office's ability to work with other departments has diminished at the same time. Canada's access regime is so dysfunctional, according to Legault, that the RCMP has actually stopped responding to access requests entirely and the Department of National Defence has stated that it will require 1,100 days to complete a single request it has been working on.[7]

Not dissimilar to her predecessors, Ms. Legualt's recipe to improve Canada's outdated access laws include, giving the commissioner order-making power, legislated periodic reviews of the statute, removing the many exceptions and exemptions in the act to promote disclosure, insisting on record creation duties that take into account the new digital realties, and, most topical, the extension of the act to cover Parliament, including parliamentary administration, and ministers' offices. In other jurisdictions, including British Columbia, Alberta, Ontario, and Quebec, the information commissioner has order-making power. The federal commissioner has no power to compel, only to recommend. This must be corrected.

Despite this increase in information that the commissioner must deal with, as more and more decision making is made at the cabinet table and in the Prime Minister's Office, the public has less access to this, crucial information, as those institutions are statutorily exempt from access to information laws.

The current high-profile, ineligible expenses scandals involving four senators highlight why the omission of Parliament, the democratic seat of government, is such a glaring flaw in Canada's access laws. Certainly all institutions funded by taxpayer dollars ought to be open to public scrutiny through access to information laws. The Canadian Journalists for Free Expression have marvelled that "[i]t is hard to comprehend how two of the most significant institutions in the functioning of Canadian democracy are not subject to access to information inquiries." In fact, the institutions outside of access to information's reach are not only the two houses of Parliament; they include also the cabinet and the Prime Minister's Office — all of these excluded institutions play a vital role in our democracy and information under their respective control is critical to transparency and to open government.[8]

According to the Canadian Journalists for Free Expression:

> In the wake of the Senate Scandal, it is all the more apparent that the House of Commons, the Senate, and the cabinet should be made subject to the Access to Information Act so that the cleasing effect of sunlight might reduce corruption and deceit in these corridors.

It is conceivable that if Canada's access laws applied to parliamentary institutions, including the Senate, the Senate Expenses Scandal may not have occurred, or would have been uncovered much earlier, with the resultant smaller cost to the taxpayer. Certainly, MPs and senators would be less likely to be creative with their expense accounts if there was a reasonable prospect that their schemes would be uncovered. Transparency is an effective deterrent to individuals inclined to treat taxpayers disrespectfully.

Many parliamentarians claim that it is unnecessary to extend the Access to Information Act to include them as they can post information and expenses voluntarily. Indeed, the voluntary posting of expenses has become one the current buzzwords inside of the Ottawa Bubble. However, if Parliament is serious about increased openness and transparency, it must not only proactively disclose much more information regarding our expenses and allocations, we must subject ourselves to the regime created under the Access to Information Act.

In the thirty years since we have had access laws, a maturing democracy should result in an expansion of government disclosure. Although some government has opened up through voluntary and proactive disclosure, the amount of information available as of right now, through access to information laws, is actually shrinking, as the list of exemptions has doubled since the act's inception.

The problem with proactive disclosure is that it is often voluntary, not mandatory or required by statute. In such a system, there is no method of independently verifying that the voluntary proactive disclosure is accurate or complete.

If any good is to come out of the Senate Expenses Scandal, it is that the entire debacle has shone light on Canada's antiquated access to information legislation. As both the PMO and the Senate are not covered by the act, it has become clear that Canadians (and the RCMP) will have to look elsewhere if they are ever to uncover details as to who knew what, when, and what was promised in exchange for a $90,000 cheque to a sitting legislator.

❖

Most experts agree that a comprehensive approach and over-haul of the act is preferable to piecemeal access amendments. However, convinced that the government was never going to overhaul the act in any comprehensive manner, I opted for that, not recommended, piecemeal approach.

My private member's bill, C-461, The CBC and Public Service Disclosure and Accountability Act, had two purpos-es. First, it attempted to correct a much maligned and fre-quently litigated section of the Access to Information Act regarding the public broadcaster. Section 68.1 of the act indi-cates that the act does not apply to documents under control of the CBC "that [relate] to its journalistic, creative, or pro-gramming activities, other than information that relates to its general administration."

This awkwardly worded provision was used repeatedly by the CBC to deny access requests based on the exclusion for journalistic, creative, or programming activities. The CBC argued that the words "this act does not apply" are self-explanatory and if the act does not apply, the rights of appeal and the information commissioner's processes and powers of review are equally inapplicable.

Both the Federal Court and the Federal Court of Appeal disagreed, but conceded that the section was "not a model of clarity" because it created an exclusion and then created an ex-ception to the exclusion for purely administrative documents.

Bill C-461, as originally drafted, would have repealed Section 68.1 and removed the blanket exclusion, but allowed a discretionary exemption based on an injury test. If CBC could demonstrate prejudice by the release of journalistic, creative, or programming documents, they could deny disclosure. However, if there was no injury or prejudice, disclosure should be the result. Moreover, the information commissioner's unfettered right of review would be re-established.

The government, however, was persuaded to amend C-461 in committee to provide an absolute exclusion for journalistic source documents. Although I am certainly in principle supportive of protecting the identity of confidential journalistic sources, I believe that would have easily been accomplished by the CBC routinely satisfying the prejudice test. However, the government amendments removed the commissioner's powers of review regarding access to these sensitive documents.

Furthermore, the mechanics of the amendment were once again awkward — an exclusion, subject to an exception, had been replaced by a discretionary exemption, subject to an exclusion. The inevitable result of this awkward wording would be more, not less, litigation.

The second, and more reported, aspect of C-461 was an amendment to the Privacy Act to allow for the disclosure of specific salaries and actual responsibilities of government employees under the Access to Information Act. The bar originally chosen was that of the lowest level of deputy minister, or approximately $188,000.

However, in a much publicized manoeuvre members of the Access and Privacy Committee were instructed by PMO staffers to gut the bill and move the salary benchmark to above the highest possible level of a deputy minister, or approximately $444,000. This amendment would guarantee that no deputy minister, or any member of a department, would be covered by the salary disclosure requirement. The only federal servants who earn more than $444,000 are the CEOs of some of the Crown corporations and possibly a few of the full-time chairs of arms-length agencies and tribunals such as the Canadian Radio-television and Telecommunications Commission (CRTC).

The government's deliberate evisceration of this, admittedly piecemeal attempt to improve Canada's access laws made a mockery of its claims to be a proponent of government transparency. Sadly, it was also indicative of the government's approach to transparency and openness generally.

Why did the government not support my attempts to provide for specific salary disclosure for federal public servants? The answer is painfully simple. The Conservative government was concerned that a whole series of bad news stories would be written once it was disclosed how much it was paying some of its top civil servants and how many federal bureaucrats were above that $188,000 threshold.

But it gets worse. Civil servants at the upper echelons of the federal public service are entitled to "at risk pay," or what is commonly referred to as a bonus. Under Canada's existing access laws, a broad range of salaries may be disclosed at all salary levels, but not a word can be mentioned about the bonus. The government is deliberately shielding from the public access to information concerning the up to $124,000 that a deputy minister can make in a performance bonus.

Sadly, the access to information advocated in my bill was replaced by an amendment that perpetuated government secrecy, an amendment made to prevent the government from having to defend how much it pays its mandarins in terms of salaries and bonuses.

This brings us to nub of the problem. Openness is in the public interest, it is in the media's interest, in the interest of academics and also MPs. Openness and transparency is crucial for Members of Parliament, the media and the public in holding their government to account. However, transparency is seldom, if ever, in the government's interest. The more the government discloses publicly, the more it will have to defend. A government that discloses nothing will have nothing to defend.

As Sydney Linden, Ontario's first information commissioner said, "It's not easy to create and sustain an effective FOI law. Secrecy is inherently attractive to government and being held accountable requires courage. Governments need strong leaders who appreciate and accept FOI law as a key component of our democratic system, not as an annoyance that needs to be damaged controlled."[9]

Sunshine is the best disinfectant.[10] For Canadians to hold their government to account, something that is fundamental to democracy, they must have access to information about what government is doing. Knowledge is power and holding to account demands that knowledge and information is available to the public. Holding to account leads to the establishment of trust, trust that there is proper stewardship over public resources. Opacity, however, leads to mistrust, or at least suspicion that there is not proper stewardship over public resources.

Canadians want, expect, and deserve more transparency in government, not less. They want access to accurate and complete information on issues that affect them. They want to know what is behind a government policy, what information was considered, how tax dollars are spent, and how spending decisions are made. Access to information legislation gives citizens a legal framework to obtain those answers regarding how their government is managing the affairs of state and how it is spending their tax dollars. Properly functioning access regimes result in citizens who are better informed and more fully engaged in participatory democracy.

Former Ontario attorney-general Ian Scott stated, while announcing his province's first access law, "When there is true openness in government, we will have a society that is trustful of its government, not fearful of it. We will have a society that is enlightened by information and able to make thoughtful choices as to the future shape of our society."[11]

There is nothing more fundamental to democracy than an informed public.

12.

THE MEDIA: IF IT BLEEDS, IT LEADS

Nothing is more important to a democracy than an informed electorate.

The statement is both trite and profound. Whatever else we may say about the sad state of our democracy, at least once every five years the electorate gets the opportunity to renew the country's leadership. Forty-one times in Canada's nearly-150 year history, Canadians have had the opportunity to choose who will represent them in Parliament.

It is an important decision, and prudence and care must be taken to ensure the choice is made appropriately. An electorate needs to be informed if it is to fulfill the democratic mandate bestowed upon it. For democracy to work properly, the electorate must be able to make an informed evaluation of the job the incumbent government has done. In democracy, the electorate must be able to compare the incumbents to the platforms of all of the alternatives.

Accordingly, the media, although not formally part of government, serves as an important check on government. Indeed, as the formal institutions within government are increasingly failing so miserably at providing a meaningful check on the actual government, society has been forced to become more and more reliant on outside institutions, such as the media and, as we shall examine in the next chapter, the courts, to pick up the slack.

In totalitarian regimes, the media is controlled by the state. In a democracy, however, the media is free (at least in theory), and through it the electorate should be able to gain access to accurate information about the government, information that plays an integral role in the system of checks and balances. Public access to verifiable information, gathered by voluntary suppliers of the information, is critical. Accurate information empowers the public by providing the necessary tools for participation in the political process.

A well-functioning media will both lead and contribute to an informed debate on important issues. A dysfunctional media will distort information, leading to potentially calamitous results.

How good is the modern media at holding government to account?

Good and bad. It is certainly doing a better job than most MPs; but it is not as effective as it could be, and it is certainly not as effective as society needs it to be.

In determining the effectiveness of the media, the first problem is defining exactly what term "media" refers to. There is the broadcast media, print media, digital media, multimedia, alternative or underground media, and, now, social media. The second problem stems from the first: the complete fracturing of the media and media market. Since there has been a complete fracturing of the mass media, which includes all of the above types of media, and an even more pronounced fracturing of the audience, it has become very difficult to assess how good a job the media is doing in informing the citizenry about the government and the issues of the day.

Growing up in Melville, Saskatchewan, in the 1960s and 1970s, we received one television signal, the CBC, and three AM radio stations. We did not get CTV until 1978, and U.S. cable channels did not arrive until 1980. A half-century later, I have access to hundreds of television stations and dozens of FM radio stations catering to every possible music taste from classic rock to hip hop to dance to modern country to easy listening to Christian rock. On top of all that, I can also access social media: websites, bloggers, and Twitter.

With so many choices, two realities present themselves: the media is a tough business and any one provider of information will find challenges in finding an adequate audience; also, with so many options, the public has an increasingly difficult time knowing where to turn to find "news."

Given this situation, it is clear that no news anchor will ever again enjoy an audience the size of Lloyd Robertson's when he hosted *The National* from 1970–1976. Media providers now struggle in a fierce competition to attract viewers who have hundreds of media options. The simple business reality is that all of these media outlets must attract viewers or readers in order to attract advertisers. Ratings and circulation are the variables that determine if a media source flourishes or if it hands out pink slips. With the proliferation of different media sources, it has become more and more difficult for individual outlets to succeed. Almost all have been cutting back, making do with less. The newspaper business has been hit especially hard in recent years by the latter reality.

There remain, of course, good media sources. And, of course, there are still fine journalists. I know many political reporters both in Edmonton and in Ottawa. They are, without a doubt, some of the brightest, hardest working political minds in the Edmonton and Ottawa Bubbles. In fact, I generally prefer the company of journalists over politicians. I find my media contacts more objective, generally better informed, and certainly more humble than my few remaining political friends.

There are great journalists working in all of the media. There is great investigative journalism done in print media, both newspapers and newsmagazines. Canada has a bevy of talented political columnists representing every conceivable bias and political persuasion. Broadcast media does a generally good job in breaking news, often in real time; and investigative and documentary programs do yeoman's work in providing detailed background and analysis. Professional social media bloggers, meanwhile, provide both facts and analysis, react much quicker, and post updates more frequently than their print media counterparts.

If many journalists, individually, excel at good journalism, why does the media as a collective generally do such an inadequate job of keeping the public informed?

The answer has much more to do with the needs, interests and patience of the audience than it does with the quality of the journalism. The electorate is mostly disengaged, especially between elections, and has a short attention span, and many media options. For the most part, it is seeking entertainment, distraction, not critical, thoughtful investigative reporting and analysis, and so most quality journalism falls on deaf ears. Media outlets need to maintain an audience to stay in business, so knowing that there will always be an audience for the salacious and the sensational, they pursue it. The result: tabloid-style news programs where if it bleeds, it leads.

As an illustration: an interesting story could be written concerning the incredible technical developments that have occurred that promote aeronautic safety; however, a million planes landing safely are not newsworthy. A single passenger plane tragically crashing, however, will be both front-page news and the lead story on national newscasts.

My first political boss, Premier Ralph Klein, himself a former political reporter at Calgary city hall, used to say that the traditional five Ws of journalism (who, what, when, where, and why) have been displaced in the modern media era by the 5Cs (although, frequently, he would only be able to list three or four of them).

According to Klein's "5C" theory, the media will be interested in a story it involves one or more of the following:

- Controversy
- Conflict
- Chaos
- Confusion
- Confrontation

The more Cs that are included in the story, the more likely it is that it will get written and produced and the more public interest it will generate.

The five o'clock cable political talk shows in Canada certainly seem to like exploiting this formula. On any given program, one or more panels will be convened comprised either of MPs from each of the major political parties or a panel of partisan "insiders." The insiders are generally party strategists, usually from either a lobbying or strategic communications firm, but clearly identified with one of the political parties and dispatched specifically to defend and promote it.

The format is designed specifically around a current controversy; pitting partisans against one another invariably invokes conflict. However, rarely will there be a respectful discussion providing accurate information in a context to allow for informed debate of alternate viewpoints. It is much more likely that the panelists will be talking past each other, cutting each other off and talking over one other. Frequently a combatant will be heard to say: "I didn't cut you off when you were speaking and I would appreciate the same courtesy."

The segment will frequently descend into confusion, and occasionally even chaos.

I find these panels both uninstructive and, frequently, painful to watch. The MPs are even more insufferable than the partisan pundits. However, the fact that we see such panels presented just about every day confirms the fact that the producers believe they have value, or more accurately, an audience.

The media will frequently feed the beast of conflict and controversy further by falsely concluding that dissent or disagreement within a political party is indicative of the unravelling of the particular party, or a sign of weak leadership. Dissent and debate is healthy in a democracy and should be encouraged rather than torqued up to create a story, when in actuality none exists.

Sadly, as is all too often the case, ratings drive content.

The majority of viewers will almost always prefer to hear about Justin Bieber's latest shenanigan, Kim Kardashian's pregnancy, or why Jodi Arias murdered her boyfriend, over the intricacies of the Bank of Canada's interest rate policy.

This is true notwithstanding the fact that the former has absolutely no effect or bearing on the viewer's life while the latter may determine if the viewers can find job or keep their jobs, or whether they can afford mortgages, new houses, or to pay off their credit cards.

❖

After the 2011 election, I enhanced my social media presence by trying to post a weekly blog. Over time, I have been able to grow a modest following. However, I soon discovered that I could exponentially increase the size of my audience if the topic touched one or more of the five Cs.

Whereas a thoughtful piece on the unreliability, and potential for manipulation, of crime statistics or on the need for more transparency in government would generate little to no interest outside of my catchment, anything overtly critical of the government would increase my audience and frequently attract the attention of the mainstream media. For example, when I criticized the minister of national defence for mishandling the F-35 procurement, or, more notably, when I criticized ministerial opulence in a blog post entitled "Of Orange Juice and Limos," I received wide national broadcast and print media coverage. Although unfortunate, the reality is that there is nothing particularly newsworthy about a backbencher's thoughtful piece on the government's most recent budget. The conflict and internal controversy of a government backbencher criticizing or even questioning a minister, however, is salacious enough to attract the national press gallery.

Similarly, I seriously underestimated the media interest that my resignation from the Conservative caucus would generate. I anticipated local and regional coverage but was not prepared for the sudden attention from the National Press Gallery.

After I notified the local Conservative riding association, the Speaker of the House, the chief government whip, and the PMO, I posted the decision on Twitter. The reaction was swift, unpredictable, and overwhelming. Both the Ottawa office phone and my Blackberry rang and buzzed continually for at least the next hour. I took no calls and only responded by email and Twitter, letting people know that there would be media availability the next day at 11a.m. at my St. Albert constituency office.

I decided that I would make myself available to the local media only, primarily because it was important to me that my constituents understood my decision and the reasons behind it. I honestly did not anticipate any national interest in my caucus resignation, much less the overwhelming amount that I, in fact, received.

I had to shut off my Blackberry because it was still buzzing at midnight and I had to get up at 5 a.m. to catch a 7 a.m. flight from Ottawa to Edmonton. However, my plan to speak only to the local media was thwarted when Laura Peyton from CBC staked out the Departures level of the Ottawa Airport.

When I landed in Edmonton, I had no idea what lay in store for me. When I turned my phone on, I had dozens of messages, but the only one that I was interested in was the one from my staff notifying me that there were two camera crews waiting for me at the Arrivals level. Fortunately, a tenant from our floor in St. Albert was at the airport to meet a family member's plane. Apparently, my resignation from caucus was all he could listen to on talk radio on his trip out to the airport, so he knew who the media was waiting for. He alerted my office and my office alerted me. Since I have been in and out of the Edmonton airport hundreds of times, I certainly know how to get to the parkade without going anywhere near the Arrivals level when necessary. That knowledge certainly helped me that day.

However, I was perplexed. I had scheduled media availability for 11 a.m. Why, I wondered, was it so important for the media to talk to me that they would drive all the way out to the Edmonton airport to meet me getting off my plane at a quarter to ten? Apparently, in such a competitive media market, media outlets drive ratings by being the first to report some aspect or detail of a story, or by getting the first interview.

I drove into downtown St. Albert, still unaware of the breadth of interest in the story of my caucus resignation. As I turned the corner onto Perron Street, I saw four satellite trucks there, causing traffic congestion, which is rarity in suburban St. Albert. The two-storey office building containing my office was bursting with activity; technicians were bustling around, distributing thick black cables, running them from my second floor office down the stairs, out the doors, and into the satellite trucks.

All of the networks had assembled; as well, both local and metro papers, news radio, and the Canadian Press were all represented. Al three cable news networks broadcasted the press conference live, and Global, not having a twenty-four-hour news network, went live in several markets. My resignation from the Conservative caucus was pre-empting *Days of Our Lives*!

Months later, the resignation of two longer-serving Alberta MPs, the Honourable Ted Menzies and Brian Jean, would be announced by press release.

Why such intense media coverage of a relatively obscure MP's resignation from the Conservative caucus?

It was the five Cs. Nobody had ever voluntarily left a Stephen Harper–led caucus. Garth Turner, Bill Casey, and Helena Guergis had all been expelled, but before Rathgeber, nobody had ever rejected the powers that be. By so doing, I had put at least three of the five Cs in play. The Controversy was over the gutting of my private member's bill. There was express Conflict between myself and the PMO staffers and Minister Rona Ambrose, all of whom were calling for me to resign my seat. There was Confusion as to what it all meant first to caucus unity, which had already been tested by Mark Warawa and the "backbench spring," and also what it meant for my personal political future.

Involve three or more of the five Cs in a news story, and you can pre-empt *Days of Our Lives*!

❖

Although not planned, my interactions with the media following my resignation from the Conservative caucus followed what is a conventional media strategy for governments and politicians — employing the media to get one's message out. Advertising is expensive, but a positive media story is free and is guaranteed to reach a substantial audience. This relationship works for the media also: journalists require credible government sources to write timely, accurate, and interesting stories.

The potential for a symbiotic relationship exists. The Harper Conservative government, however, has developed such an adversarial relationship with the National Press Gallery that no such mutually beneficial relationship is possible. The Prime Minister's Office likes to get its message out unfiltered, and accordingly will frequently attempt to circumvent the media. The prime minister rarely will hold a press conference inside the Ottawa Bubble. When he does meet with the media, it is a tightly scripted event — two questions in English and two questions in French is the standard. Journalists have been punished by the Comms director for attempting to ask a question when not on the "approved list." Recently, PMO Comms has developed podcasts, called 24/Seven, which allows the prime minister to get an unfiltered message out to the public without media interception or intervention.

In my view, Prime Minister Harper distrusts the media because it is an institution that he cannot control. Through highly scripted media conferences, generally a minimum of one hundred kilometres from Parliament Hill, the Prime Minister's Office attempts to control an otherwise independent institution.

So adversarial is the relationship between the federal government and the national media that the Conservative Party is actually using the adversarial relationship in it fundraising efforts. A CPC fundraising letter suggests that the party needs donations to counter the biased and negative news coverage it is receiving from the Senate Expenses Scandal. This is certainly an unusual use of the strategy of using the media to help promote your cause!

❖

As I write this, without any doubt the two biggest political stories in Canada are the Senate/PMO Expenses Scandal and the self-destruction of Mayor Rob Ford. I think they register 4.5 and 5 respectively the 5C scale. Unlike the latest gossip surrounding Miley Cyrus, there is an obvious public interest in both political stories. But undoubtedly it is the more salacious aspects of the stories, in addition to the constant twists, turns and new developments that keep both stories interesting.

There is clear public interest. In October 2014, voters of Toronto will be called upon to pass judgment on the performance of their mayor, and a year later all of Canada will render a verdict on the trustworthiness, integrity, honesty, and leadership skills of Prime Minister Harper and his government. However, I would argue that the public's interest in either story greatly exceeds the actual public interest.

Outside of Toronto, most Canadians do not have a direct interest in the Rob Ford train wreck. However, we certainly find it interesting. On the other hand, although all Canadians have a legitimate interest in the ethical standards of senators and PMO staffers, I suspect it is actually the more surreal and scandalous aspects of the story that keep it interesting. Add a healthy dose of *schadenfreude* and the public's undivided attention will be captured.

Of course, a story that would have a much more direct bearing on millions of Canadians will hold much less of their interest. A well-researched story on the benefits to the economy of lowering consumption taxes like the GST versus the benefits of creating boutique income tax credits will never capture the public's imagination to the same extent as Anthony Weiner.

The complexity of an economic analysis of various taxation options is not easy to present in most media formats. It's complicated, and requires concentration and a long attention span. The reader or viewer has to ponder and digest the respective arguments. It is no way amenable to the seven-second sound bite. Conversely, there is nothing complicated about taking in the information that a congressman or mayoralty candidate has taken inappropriate and bizarre photos of himself. Simple sells.

Besides the public's tendency to want the news dumbed down for mass consumption, there are other factors which compromise the media's ability to hold government to account. Many newsrooms are overworked and understaffed. Print media has been especially susceptible to mass layoffs in recent years. Lack of resources, in addition to inflexible deadlines, has resulted in junior reporters frequently lifting their stories directly from press releases that have been sent to the newsroom. Reliance on the daily diet of photo ops, vague platitudes, and bland policy statements sent directly by government is not real journalism. When that occurs, the media becomes an extension of the government's communications branches rather than a check on government. Public relations is not news.

Even reporters who go out in the field to collect a story can be abetting a government if they are dependent on that government. In Iraq and Afghanistan, for example, imbedded reporters were frequently reliant on the government for safety and logistics. In such a dynamic, the subject host has an unfettered ability to show the reporter what the host wants them to see. It has been suggested that many favourable stories about the Canadian Forces involvement in the Afghan conflict were manipulated through guided tours of journalists.[1]

Finally, reporters will occasionally practise self-censorship and will pull or sanitize stories that are unflattering to reliable sources or sometimes advertisers. A journalist will risk losing a valuable and reliable source if something negatvie is written about the source. A writer must carefully weigh the cost versus the benefit of such a story.

Similarly, a publisher or producer will be most mindful of

the need for accuracy and balance in any story involving a valued advertiser.

❖

Despite all of the problems with the media outlined above, there are, as I have mentioned, many talented political journalists working today. They are hard-working and conform to high ethical standards. The problem is that they work in the same industry that produces reality TV, *Entertainment Tonight*, *TMZ*, *People* magazine, and the *National Enquirer*. Thoughtful, provocative journalism is in a fierce competition for viewers and readers. However, it is often "infotainment" that grabs the greatest number of those.

Preoccupation with "gotcha" stories, scandals, polls, and gaffes do little to lead or contribute to an informed public dialogue, but is perhaps understandable if one only considers media outlets as businesses. Private media have a fiduciary duty to their stockholders. As a result, ratings and circulation tend to drive content. Journalists face the dilemma of dumbing down their stories for a mass audience, or becoming irrelevant. The duty to inform the national dialogue will always be pitted against the drive to make a profit or, in some cases, just to survive. A good and effective media informs and educates the electorate; a poorly functioning media will misdirect attention, potentially causing irreparable damage. A good media is the conduit of both accuracy and context; it is also the antithesis of hyperbole and innuendo. More than ever, we need more good media.

A well-functioning media is critical in holding government to account. This is especially critical as all of the formal political institutions continue to fail us in so doing.

13.

JUDICIAL REVIEW: A TRUE CHECK ON GOVERNMENT POWER

Canada is now a constitutional democracy. Parliament may have been supreme at one point, but as this book has demonstrated, there has been a continual erosion of parliamentary authority in favour of executive prerogative. The supremacy of Parliament was further eroded on April 17, 1982, when Canada patriated its Constitution and expressly made all laws subject to a Charter of Rights and Freedoms.

The current government is fond of accusing the judiciary of behaving in an overtly activist manner; the courts, it declares, overreach themselves and strike down legitimate laws passed by democratically elected institutions. However, that was exactly the objective of the Charter of Rights and Freedoms; it was created so that neither Parliament nor any provincial legislature could pass any law that violates the rights protected by the Charter.

Unfortunately, given the impotency of Parliament in holding the executive to account, it has now become the function of the courts to provide a check on governmental authority, by vetting and then disallowing any laws that are not compliant with the fundamental rights enjoyed by Canadians.

For example, on December 20, 2013, the Supreme Court of Canada upheld an Ontario Court of Appeal decision in R. v. Bedford,[1] declaring three prostitution-related prohibitions were unconstitutional. Formerly, Canada had an odd legal situation; the selling of sex was not illegal, but almost everything associated with it was.

Prostitution-related activities such as keeping a common bawdy house, communicating for the purposes, and living off of the avails of prostitution forced sex workers onto the unsafe streets, prohibited meaningful vetting of prospective clients, and made it illegal to hire bodyguard drivers respectively. Bedford et al. argued persuasively that these three Criminal Code prohibitions made practising a legal trade unsafe and that this was in violation of the Canadian Charter's protection of security of the person.

Sadly, there is no shortage of evidence to support that proposition. The actions of serial killer Robert Pickton and the findings of Edmonton's Project KARE Task Force on over a dozen murdered or missing women from "at risk" lifestyles provide only a couple of the examples of why streetwalking is a dangerous, sometimes lethal, vocation.

The government's response was predictable. Not the least bit interested in harm reduction, Justice Minister Peter McKay issued a statement of disappointment. The government, he said, would "explore all possible options to ensure the criminal law continues to address the significant harms that flow from prostitution to communities, those engaged in prostitution and vulnerable persons."[2] Apparently, the justice minister did not buy the argument made in successive court rulings that it was, in actuality, the criminal law itself that caused significant harm to "those engaged in prostitution and vulnerable persons" by forcing sex workers to work solo on the streets.

The government not only disapproved of the court's rulings, it objected to the intervention of the court in the government's legislative agenda, since it is particularly suspicious of what it terms "judicial activism." Senior cabinet minister Jason Kenney's view is that "the judiciary should be restrained in the exercise of overturning a democratic consensus."[3] According to this commonly held Conservative viewpoint, Parliament should craft the laws and the courts interpret them, period. The problem with that position is that Parliament voluntarily surrendered to the courts arbitration regarding Charter compliance when the Charter of Rights and Freedoms was entrenched in the Canadian Constitution in 1982.

As a lawyer, I see no overreaching when the courts strike down a law that is offensive to the Canadian Charter of Rights and Freedoms. I take a different position, however, when the court orders the government to do something Parliament has not legislated, such as when it ordered Health Canada to provide a licence to Vancouver's Insite Facility (a safe injection site for drug users). There was no legal requirement for the government to provide this license, and in ordering it to do so the court was acting in an area where it had no proper function. The other factor that distinguishes the Insite decision from that regarding prostitution is that prostitution itself is legal, whereas possessing narcotics is not.

A check on Parliament's authority does not include writing laws; that legislative function properly belongs to Parliament. But the court is well within its function to strike down laws that are non-compliant with the Constitution. That is part of the court's recognized and legitimate role of providing judicial review and interpreting the law.

The Supreme Court expressly gave Parliament one year to craft, if it chooses, Charter-compliant restrictions regarding the sex trade. Lobbying was already well underway when reactions to the judgment were being collected. Terri-Jean Bedford and other organized sex workers believe Parliament should not take up the invitation, thus leaving all matters, save for trafficking and employing underage prostitutes, legal. There is strong opposition to this approach from church groups and from some within the Conservative Party, especially the social conservative flank. The government's response to R. v. Bedford was tabled in the House in June 2014. Bill C-36 adopts an approach championed by anti-trafficking Conservative MP Joy Smith and referred to as "the Nordic model." This approach punishes the purchasers of sex but not the sellers. Premised on the belief that women who participate in the trade do so on a non-voluntary basis, the Nordic model advocates prosecuting johns, thus theoretically reducing demand and ensuring that already marginalized women are not re-victimized.

This approach is opposed by Ms. Bedford, who believes sanctions against purchasers will still force the industry underground, thereby doing nothing to promote sex-worker safety. I am not convinced that the government's legislation will fare any better with the courts either. The chief justice stated that Parliament can regulate against nuisance "but not at the cost of the health, safety, and lives of prostitutes."

Moreover, the liberty of purchasers will also attract Charter protection; if one can be jailed or otherwise punished for purchasing sex, which is not illegal in Canada, the Nordic model becomes constitutionally suspect. I am searching for a product that is legal to sell in Canada but illegal to purchase.[4]

It seems counterintuitive to accept the selling of sex but not the purchase. The libertarian in me believes that the only practicable solution is regulation of the industry. If consenting participants were licensed, health and safety concerns could be addressed. Trafficked or other involuntary participants would not be granted licences. Hopefully, a legal market would reduce demand for an illegal one. This is the approach that Canada takes with respect to other morally challenging products such as tobacco, alcohol, and even exotic dancing. Imperfect in all instances, but it is likely preferable to any attempts at outright prohibition or to the opposite: unregulated anarchy.

I admit to be not entirely comfortable with this approach, but as a legislator, I must examine a bigger picture than my own moral compass. I must also consult extensively with my constituents, many of whom I am certain will be equally uncomfortable. That is the important difference between the approach undertaken by the judiciary versus the analysis undertaken by politicians. While the latter must consider personal philosophies and political ramifications, the former is only concerned with objective analysis and judicial precedent. Ideally, it would be parliamentarians who address these socially challenging issues. But, its inability, and sometimes unwillingness, to do so means, unfortunately, that the task fall increasingly upon the courts.

The approach taken by the Supreme Court in "Bedford" was not entirely dissimilar to the approach taken by the same court twenty-five years ago in R. v. Morgentaler.[5] The SCC held in 1988 that the situation regarding abortion that existed in

Canada at the time, a hodgepodge of inconsistent access-to-abortion procedures provided by disjointed collection of therapeutic abortion committees, was a violation of a woman's security of the person.

The court specifically invited Parliament to draft a law that was more reasonable and Charter-compliant. The Mulroney government attempted this daunting task and actually got legislation passed in the House of Commons only to see it narrowly defeated in the Senate.

And therein lies the problem: Parliament's inability to craft an acceptable law regulating a woman's access to therapeutic abortion has created a huge void in Canadian law, which makes Canada unique among Western democracies.

When Parliament cannot, or will not, update its laws to adapt to society's changing norms, beliefs, and values, it will fall upon the courts to do so, either by expressly striking down constitutionally offensive statutes or by directing the government to do something it has neglected to do or chosen not to. This was the situation regarding the court's insistence that the government assist with harm reduction for chronic drug users using safe injection sites. It was also the case in Vriend v. Alberta,[6] where the courts ordered Alberta to amend its human rights legislation to include protection for homosexuals against discrimination.

Although both striking down offensive statutes and mandating government action will earn the courts criticism for inappropriate judicial activism, only the latter examples demonstrate actual overreach by the judiciary. Courts, in my view, ought to strike down laws passed by legislatures that infringe the Charter, but they should be reticent to order the government to legislate in an area the legislature has chosen not to. Courts are not legislators, and, therefore, while they may properly vet statutes to ensure constitutional compliance, they should not, in my view, replace or second-guess legislators.

It is for this reason that the Insite decision is problematic, although I found the process more troubling than the result. Under the Controlled Drug and Substances Act,[7] the minister of health has discretion to exempt the possession prohibition of a drug for "medical or scientific purpose or [if it] is otherwise in the public interest."

The issue is not so much whether harm reduction is or is not in the public interest; the issue is whether the minister's discretion is permissive or mandatory. The Supreme Court, in holding that Insite be granted an exemption, stated that the refusal to issue a permit was a "arbitrary and grossly disproportionate in its effects and hence not in accordance with the principles of fundamental [j]ustice."

The court concluded that "the effect of denying the services of Insite to the population it serves is grossly disproportionate to any benefit that Canada might derive from presenting a uniform stance on the possession of narcotics." But in my view, it is Parliament, not the courts, that should weigh the relative merits of narcotic control versus harm reduction for addicts. Both are valid policy objectives, but it is the legislature, not the courts, who ought to rank and choose between competing policy priorities.

It is largely section 15, or the section of the Charter that sets forth the right to "equal protection and equal benefit of the law without discrimination," that has been used by the courts to expand the role of government and force it do something it may not otherwise have been inclined to do. This is the genesis of the criticism of the courts for engaging in judicial activism.

But the irony lost on critics of judicial activism is that if legislatures and governments did their jobs properly, the courts would not need to intervene. Certainly it is incumbent on governments not to pass unconstitutional laws. But equally axiomatic, legislatures must keep up with changing values. Who better to reflect changing societal norms than parliamentarians and legislators periodically elected by the citizens and accountable to them?

Undoubtedly, societal values regarding gay marriage, reproductive rights, and prostitution change over time. If legislators refuse to update laws to keep up with changing mores, that function by necessity will fall upon the courts. The Charter of Rights and Freedoms does not give the courts the power to write laws, but it gives the judiciary the ability, and the responsibility, to measure any particular law against a higher law, the Constitution of Canada.

There is a fine but important line between judicial activism and legislative inaction. This was amply demonstrated by Parliament's inaction regarding the updating of the laws surrounding prostitution; for example, while providing no prohibition against prostitution itself, the laws regarding activities associated with prostitution endangered the lives of people working in a legal trade. The risks were actually increased by the Criminal Code prohibitions!

Critics of judicial activism must come to grips with the reality that if Parliament and governments did a better job of passing constitutional laws and updating them to reflect changing societal values, there would be no, or at least less, cause for the courts to intervene. Moreover, and by logical extension, if the courts were as deferential as many parliamentarians request, the rights and freedoms guaranteed to Canadians by their Constitution would have no protectors whatsoever.

The list of changing norms, beliefs, and values that legislators have ignored, or were politically incapable of responding to, is growing. The issue of same-sex marriage provides a concrete illustration of how Parliament's initial reluctance to respond to a changing value was dealt with by the courts and then how the courts' rulings finally spurred Parliament to act. Initially, the government refused to change the legislation concerning marriage in order to permit same-sex marriages. However, when the courts ruled that bans on same-sex marriages infringed the equality rights protected by the Canadian Charter, it became obvious that Parliament would legalize same sex marriage, which it did in 2005.

❖

The contest between the government and the courts over so-called judicial activism has recently involved several government measures dealing with the sentencing of convicted criminals. A number of these tough-on-crime or "safe street and safe community" initiatives have come under judicial scrutiny. These criminal law amendments (some of which, it should be noted, were passed while I was on the Justice Committee), involve such measures as requiring minimum mandatory sentences for possession of an illegal firearm or taking away a judge's discretion to waive a victim fine surcharge. Many of these have been struck down or ignored by trial courts, or have appeals pending against them.

The issue of judicial discretion was a hotly contested matter while the laws removing it were being debated. Judicial discretion is seen as related to judicial activism, since, as critics of the judiciary argue, courts that use their discretion in a manner that was unintended (from the critic's perspective) are acting as judicial activists.

In defence of judicial discretion, sociologists, criminologists, defenders of those involved in the criminal process such as the John Howard Society, and even occasionally a retired criminal court judge would invariably appear before the Justice Committee to argue that every situation is unique. According to them, there is no such thing as one-size-fits-all criminal justice, and, therefore, judges, the argument goes, must maintain a certain degree of discretion to waive a minimum mandatory sentence in order to accommodate unique circumstances or to waive a victim fine surcharge when a defendant is truly indigent.

Although I generally agree with the concept of allowing some judicial discretion, it is the abuse of discretion that makes Conservatives outraged and makes justice ministers want to intervene. The public is similarly outraged when it reads that an individual convicted of sexual assault is sentenced to house arrest. This sentence seems irreconcilable with that given to another offender, who, similarly convicted of sexual assault, receives seven years in the penitentiary.

However, reading newspaper headlines rarely allows an armchair quarterback to mete out appropriate justice. How serious was the assault? Was there some sort of pre-existing relationship between the accused and the victim? Did the accused have a previous record? What are the accused's prospects for rehabilitation? These are all very relevant questions, and only the trial judge will be familiar enough with all of the relevant circumstances to determine whether or not deviation from standard sentencing guidelines is warranted.

Although there seems to be a case that can be made for judicial discretion; however, nobody ever seems to argue in favour of judicial discretion to waive a sentence at the maximum end of the allowed sentencing range. Both the minimum and maximum sentence upon conviction for first degree murder in Canada is life imprisonment, with no eligibility of parole for twenty-five years. A trial judge has absolutely no discretion to impose any other sentence. However, I have never heard either judges or advocates argue in favour of allowing deviation from that sentence to impose capital punishment or flogging in an "appropriate circumstance," for example in the case of a particularly callous and heinous murder. This inconsistency would appear to weaken the argument in favour of judicial discretion. Without a doubt, if a trial judge attempted to impose a sentence in excess of the maximum permitted by the Criminal Code, an appellate court would appropriately strike the illegal sentence down.

However, the difference between varying from a maximum and a minimum sentence is that the Charter of Rights and Freedoms ensures the rights of citizens, not the interests of government, police, or prosecutors. Accordingly, both an attempted deviation from a maximum sentence, in all situations, and automatic compliance with a seemingly harsh or otherwise inappropriate minimum mandatory sentence, will both attract Charter scrutiny.

In most circumstances, Parliament will provide a range of appropriate sentences. But where there is no range, or when the bottom of the range is either inappropriate or unduly harsh, the courts will measure the prescribed sentence against the accused's Charter-protected rights. For some, this kind of judicial review is offensive. In fact, for some even judicial rejection of legislation that does not comply with the Charter is offensive. However, such criticisms of the courts for striking down non-Charter compliant laws are misplaced. Judicial activism in its truest sense only occurs when a court orders the government to do something (Insite) or when it writes words into a statute that the legislature chose not to include (Vriend).

When a court is accused of judicial activism for merely striking down non-complaint statutes, the critics are really arguing that courts have no role in reviewing statutes. But this was a role that was voluntarily ceded to the courts when Parliament and nine provincial legislatures included a Charter of Rights in the 1982 patriated Constitution.

It is exactly because non-lawyers in the federal cabinet, including the prime minister, have such an imprecise definition of judicial activism that they are frequently and mistakenly critical of the judiciary as being activist. The distinction between judicial activism and judicial review is lost on many non-lawyers, but it is a critical distinction.

The current government has now appointed over half of the justices sitting on the Supreme Court and has had eight years to fill the superior and appellate courts of the provinces with deferential justices. The fact that the government continues to complain about judicial activism, even from Conservative-appointed judges, is perhaps indicative of the government's misunderstanding of the concept.

❖

I was part of the 2011 Supreme Court Selection Panel and I consider this function the most important role that I fulfilled as a Conservative MP. The prime minister is constitutionally entitled to make Supreme Court appointments, but he undertook to allow an all-party committee to vet prospective names and compose a short list, from which he would make his final selection(s).

Although the panel was advisory in nature, and was politically controlled as a result of the Conservatives constituting a majority of the members on the committee, the committee still served as an important mechanism to vet prospective candidates. However, the mechanism to appoint justices to the Supreme Court, although evolving, is awkward. Whereas candidates to all superior courts are vetted by a provincial judicial advisory council comprised of judges, lawyers, and lay persons, the list of prospective candidates for appointment to the Supreme Court is compiled by the Department of Justice and then vetted by the committee of Parliament.

The Department of Justice consults with members of the courts and the bars from the province in which the Supreme Court vacancy exists, but the list is drafted by the government and is kept top secret. As a result, there is actually greater opportunity for political manipulation in Supreme Court selections than in lower court appointments.

This awkward procedure produced an unbelievable result in that for the most recent Supreme Court of Canada (SCC) appointment the justice selected, Justice Marc Nadon, was deemed ineligible to sit as a Quebec judge by the SCC, because he came not directly from a Quebec court but from the Federal Court of Appeal. The justice minister has continually attempted to defend the attempted appointment, leading to the suspicion that Justice Nadon was always the government's preferred choice, regardless of the awkward selection process. Certainly, a more functional selection process would identify and eliminate candidates with potential eligibility issues.

The prime minister seems quite distrustful of lawyers generally and judges specifically. He would have tongue in cheek when he introduced his chiefs of staff, Guy Giorno and Nigel Wright, to caucus by stating they were qualified notwithstanding that they were lawyers!

I suspect that the prime minister is perhaps distrustful of lawyers because he does not understand how we think, that many believe that there are principles above political considerations, and that doing the right thing is more important than doing things right (as he sees them).

The prime minister may be distrustful of the judiciary, firstly because it is comprised of lawyers, and secondly because he cannot control it. As with the media, the judiciary is beyond the prime minister's control, and the PMO's command and control structure is incompatible with any system or group that does not answer to it or is not intimidated by it. Furthermore, as judges are appointed until age seventy-five, once appointed, they are completely immune from PMO influence and control. All of this serves to reinforce the perceived importance of ensuring that the judges appointed are compatible with the government's judicial philosophy.

The Supreme Court Selection Panel's role was to assess the names of potential nominees according to merit-based criteria. The panel was specifically interested in: professional capacity, including proficiency in the law; superior intellectual ability; analytical capacity; and writing skills.

Secondary considerations included: decisiveness; workload management; and diversity and bilingual capacity. Unofficial criteria included: judgments supporting the government's law and order agenda; and, most importantly, judicial deference.

As with everything in the Ottawa Bubble, there were attempts by the Prime Minister's Office to control the appointment process, or at least influence it. Conservative members of the committee would meet separately from the full committee with PMO staffers frequently present. This parallel selection committee assured that the vetting progressed in a manner acceptable to the PM.

The PMO has at least one full-time employee charged with vetting appointments to all courts, boards, commissions, and panels. Vetting is an amorphous term that can, and does, include philosophical and even partisan considerations. The Prime Minister's Office attempts to carefully manage the judicial appointment process because it understands that the judiciary is one of the few institutions truly independent of government. Proof of this independence can be found in the fact that the judiciary, with increasing frequency, ignores the minimum sentences and strikes down, or otherwise rules against, laws the government has passed. As a result, the current government distrusts the courts and feels that it is imperative to try to ensure that any new appointments to the bench will share the government's perspective.

The unprecedented and very public spat between the prime minister and the chief justice of the Supreme Court reinforces the lack of respect the executive has for the judiciary. The PMO's default response is always to attempt to discredit then marginalize any institution it comes into conflict with and which is cannot control.

If the government had a more precise understanding of the legitimacy of judicial review, it would be less likely to embarass itself by lashing out against a court fulfilling that legitimate fuction.

If Parliament did a better job with respect to updating laws to reflect changing societal values, in, for example, such complicated matters as harm reduction, reproductive rights, and sexual orientation, the courts could be more deferential. The fact, however, that the courts are, or at least are perceived to be, interventionist rather than deferential says more about the job Parliament and the legislatures are doing (or are not doing) than any desire for the courts to assume a larger and unintended role.

The judicial review of legislation is fundamental to a constitutional democracy. It ensures that all laws and government action are in accord with the Constitution and are Charter compliant. Critics of judicial review forget or ignore the fact that Parliament and the provincial legislatures surrendered the right of review in 1982, when they drafted and passed the Charter of Rights and Freedoms.

In a political system that is so devoid of functional checks and balances, the courts remain perhaps the only meaningful check on government power. It is for that reason that the judiciary is so frequently chastised and criticized by those who wield political power inside the Ottawa Bubble; they would prefer to do so free from interference from the one institution to whose authority they are actually subject.

14.

RESPONSIBLE GOVERNMENT IN CANADA, 1848–2014

As we saw in Chapter 2, Lord Durham's solution to an executive that was not accountable to the elected legislatures in Upper and Lower Canada was responsible government. The government and its ministers would be answerable to the legislature and each minister responsible for his or her own department.

Under the constitutional convention of responsible government, every minister of the Crown must answer to the elected legislature for the operation of the department that he or she supervises. It is the minister that is responsible for the performance and actions (or inactions) of the unelected and therefore unaccountable civil service. The concept is applicable to all ministers of the Crown, including the first minister.

It has been difficult to keep track of all of the accusations, insinuations, and conjectured conclusions that have dropped like grenades regarding who did, and knew, what with regard to the now infamous Wright/Duffy Scandal. There have been serious allegations of attempted bribery, interfering with a parliamentary (Senate) committee, and a botched cover-up in the debacle. Although Nigel Wright has never been charged for his involvement in the affair, on July 15, 2014, the RCMP laid a total of thirty-one charges against Mike Duffy, including fourteen counts each of fraud and breach of trust. As well, Duffy faces one count of bribery, fraud on the government, and breach of trust for the $90,000 cheque that he received from Wright.

Prime Minister Harper has consistently maintained (he has been very clear!) that he was not made aware of the $90,000 cheque cut by his then–chief of staff to cover Senator Mike Duffy's ineligible housing expenses.

I have consistently believed the prime minister for two reasons. The stakes are simply too high for him to have been untruthful. Moreover, PMO staffers could easily create some sort of wall to keep their boss unaware of the details for his own protection.

Although my belief in the prime minister's truthfulness appears to help exonerate the PM, in actuality it is more of an indictment of the entire PMO. That a Prime Minister's Office could act so deceptively and without the knowledge of the prime minister means that the Prime Minister's Office is accountable to no one, not even the prime minister. Moreover, there comes a point when the specific details really do not matter anymore.

Certainly, every institution is going to have some rogue operatives, and a minister cannot possibly be responsible for each and every misdeed. Nobody is going to call for a minister's resignation when an entry-level file clerk in a department is pilfering paper clips and sticky notes. But the alleged rot inside the PMO is very different. First, it has reached the very highest levels. Second, it is involving a growing number of players, all at the very highest levels of the PMO and the Conservative Party of Canada.

Thirdly, the Duffy-Wright Affair was not an isolated incident. More recently, we have learned that the then–chief of staff
pressured CPC backbencher Mark Adler to settle a potentially
politically embarrassing lawsuit with an unsavoury business associate. The PMO's meddling in a matter involving a legislator
unrelated to the government, even if politically troubling, is just
another alarming example of the executive micromanaging the
affairs of legislators.

It is no longer a sufficient response (or an accurate one) for
the PMO to claim that former chief of staff, Nigel Wright, acted alone and has taken full responsibility. It is not for a public
servant, even a highly placed one, to take responsibility for a
mess this big; that is the obligation of the supervising minister.
Given the number of senior confidants of the prime minister
that were either directly involved or at least in the know, it is no
longer acceptable to blame the entire debacle on a rogue chief of
staff, no matter how clear you are when you blame him.

There was, without a doubt, an institutional breakdown
at best, or a culture of malfeasance at worst, that allowed this
Prime Minister's Office to be blind to, or complicit in, a massive-
ly botched cover-up of a sitting legislator's expense claims. The
importance of whether it was malfeasance or mere negligence is
becoming less relevant. The prime minister is responsible to the
legislature for the operation of the PMO and the actions of its
employees. The prime minister is responsible for both the ethical
standards and the general competence of those within his office.
Nigel Wright cannot be expected to take "full responsibility" for
this fiasco; he is neither constitutionally or politically responsible.
It is the prime minister who is responsible for him and every other employee complicit in, or wilfully blind to, what was going on.

Taking responsibility for his office and offering, perhaps, a little contrition would have restored Canada's commitment to responsible government and the prime minister's reputation as a leader. Leaders lead, they do not perpetually search for scapegoats.

Clearly, the allegations of improper reimbursement for ineligible expenses, alleged interference in legislative committees studying those expense claims, and botched attempts to make it all go away represent the most serious ethical challenges to Stephen Harper's administration that have arisen to date. His refusal to take *any* responsibility for any of it, preferring to blame it all on a rogue chief of staff, whom he hired, and three senators, whom he appointed, represents an equally troubling challenge to responsible government.

❖

Sadly, I am not particularly surprised by any of this. As was outlined in the opening chapter, a government that refuses to let itself be held to account will, by definition, become unaccountable. This government has done all it can to avoid the checks and balances that would keep it accountable, a policy that it has been assisted with by the failure of some of those tasked with ensuring that accountability.

Parliament has been ineffective in holding the government to account because the government prevents Parliament from fulfilling its critical constitutional mandate. The government's tabling of omnibus bills, which prevent meaningful debate, its more recent tabling of omnibus motions, requiring all-or-nothing voting, and the constant time allocation motions it puts forward all prevent Parliament from adequately (or in any way) vetting government legislation.

The government's treatment of Question Period as a real-time infomercial similarly precludes Parliament from holding government to account. Having backbench government caucus members lob softball questions during QP allows ministers to deliver free political messaging and further restricts the ways in which the government can be held accountable. On the other hand, when the Opposition asks a real question, especially a probing one, the government's response almost invariably will be stonewalling, obfuscation, or, most troubling, an attack on the person asking the question.

In a discussion of the Senate Expenses Scandal, contrary to what parliamentary secretaries constantly opine, the real issue is *not*, "Why did the leader of the Opposition, when presented with a bribe, wait seventeen years before contacting the authorities?" Nor is it acceptable to answer a question regarding why a political party reimbursed an embattled senator's legal expenses with the response that nine years ago, when the leader of the Opposition was a Quebec MNA, his then-party paid $95,000 to settle a defamation claim on his behalf.[1]

In some other context, perhaps during a federal election, those questions might become relevant. But they in no way provide even an attempt at an answer or a legitimate government response to the actions of the government and its members in light of the allegations that have arisen as part of the Senate Expenses Scandal. Question Period is the time allocated for Parliament to hold the government to account; it is not the time for the government to hurl irrelevant barbs at MPs trying to do their jobs.

Since Parliament seems unable to hold the government to account, it is increasingly falling to other institutions and to interested Canadians to hold the government to account. The media can, and frequently does, hold government to account, and certainly, in recent years, has been more effective in doing so than Parliament. But the current government has such a negative, even dysfunctional relationship with the Ottawa press corps that the ability of the press to do its job is frequently compromised. The prime minister will rarely talk to the national media, preferring to enter and exit the House of Commons through the rear entrance.

As mentioned above, when he does hold a press conference, these events are carefully managed. "The prime minister will take two questions in English and then two in French," the Communications director will declare, stating the rules that the press must follow or be barred from future attendance. An impudent reporter from the Chinese state broadcaster recently attempted to shout a query out of turn and was threatened with being disallowed from covering the PM's Arctic tour as a punishment.[2]

When ministers scrum or when unfortunate parliamentary secretaries are dispatched to the afternoon cable political talk shows, they are provided with scripted talking points and expected to follow them. The fact that these parliamentary secretaries look foolish repeating inane talking points, as opposed to answering questions, compromises both their credibility and the press's ability to hold the government to account.

The press is of course essential for holding government to account, but ultimately it is the citizenry that must do so. A prerequisite for functioning democracy is an informed electorate. For the public to attempt to hold their government to account, functional access to information laws are required. As has been

demonstrated, although the 2006 Conservative election platform promised sweeping changes to Canada's antiquated and
"broken" access to information regime, only slight changes, such
as bringing Crown corporations under access to information
laws, have been undertake. Meanwhile, the PMO and Parliament remain exempt from the access to information regime.

As well as exempting itself from access to information laws,
the government has begun muzzling government scientists and
other employees, forbidding them from communicating information that the government does not wish the public or the
press to have access to. The government's relationship with the
academic community, meanwhile, can only be described as one
of general loathing — only the opinions and studies of those
academics deemed friendly to the government are accepted.
Indeed, the separation of the government now from anybody or
any institution intent on holding it to account is complete. As
a result, as stated earlier, Canada has been rated fifty-fifth out of
ninety-three countries studied with respect to open government
and access to information.[3] A citizen of El Salvador or Nicara-
gua can expect more transparent government than a Canadian!

The Duffy/Wright Senate Expenses Scandal is the embodi-
ment, and result, of government that refuses to let itself be held
to account.

A PMO staffed at almost every level with young, hyper-
partisan zealots, a caucus driven by blind loyalty and hopes of
self-advancement, a Parliament impotent to be a check on a
government that disrespects it, and a government with an adversarial relationship with the media all combine as the perfect
storm for an unaccountable shipwreck. A government con-
sumed with controlling all of the institutions it can, and either

destroying or discrediting the ones it cannot, will suddenly find itself operating absent any checks and balances.

Checks and balances are put into a democratic system purposely. They serve as an internal quality control system. When they break down, the system breaks down. When they are not allowed to work as intended or are manipulated, they can no longer assure quality and the result is the sad state of Canadian democracy.

Only a complete institutional failure, to borrow from the fictional *Newsroom*'s inability to prevent a false story regarding sarin gas deployment from airing, can account for rogue employees within the Prime Minister's Office interfering with a sitting legislator's expense claims, meddling with a Senate committee examining an audit, and then attempting to cover it all up. As quality control mechanisms broke down, we ceased to have any meaningful system of checks and balances.

So how did we get here? As the previous chapters have outlined, it has been a slow but discernable creep toward irresponsible government. Every time a junior staffer in the PMO distributes talking points or plants a puffball question for a backbencher, the system is breaking down. Every time an MP parrots nonsensical talking points rather than attempting to ask an actual question, he or she is contributing to institutional breakdown. Each time a parliamentary secretary goes on a cable political talk show to defend the indefensible, and every time a minister ducks a probing question in Question Period or from an inquisitive media, they are contributing to institutional breakdown.

The institutions that are charged with holding government to account fail when they are not allowed, or do not attempt, to hold government to account. The effect of inadequate quality control or complete institutional breakdown is an executive that thinks it is proper and necessary to continually meddle in the affairs of the legislature.

It starts small: read this inane talking point, vote in favour of time allocation (limiting debate); and then it graduates: you must vote against a bill that would disadvantage your constituents (such as mandated bilingualism for some government employees). Eventually, executive staffers in the Prime Minister's Office, confidant that they can control backbench caucus members, demand that blogs written by independent-thinking MPs be edited or even taken down. Satisfied that it is almost unheard of that a backbench MP, eager to move to the front bench, will defy them, the PMO will dispatch compliant MPs to a House of Commons committee to eviscerate a public sector salary disclosure bill, notwithstanding the fact that there is widespread caucus support for it and that many of those compliant MPs are privately supportive.

So complete is the feeling of near omnipotence within the young zealots at the PMO, they conclude there is nothing that they cannot control, no problem too big to fix. So, an undetermined number of them conspired with a sitting senator to fix an allegation of ineligible housing expense claims and make the problem go away. In the process, they allegedly blackmailed the legislator into going along with the scheme, interfered with a Senate committee examining an audit of the ineligible expenses, and potentially broke both the Criminal Code and the Parliament of Canada Act.

At a minimum, a "few," and perhaps as many as a dozen, highly placed members of the PMO knew what was happening and either agreed it was a good idea or were powerless to stop those so disposed. It was a complete institutional failure and the logical conclusion of a system where the political elite refuse to allow themselves to be held to account. Every time a Member of Parliament allows himself to be manipulated by a PMO puppet master, he is acquiescing in the breakdown of responsible government.

As critical as I have been of the PMO, their tactics and their methods, it is actually not them who I blame for their growing sense of omnipotence inside the Ottawa Bubble. As I said in Chapter One, as a conservative, I am inherently distrustful of government and government institutions. This is especially so regarding the ones with centralized power. So, the actions of the PMO and the executive branch of government can be considered the natural products of a system in which power is unaccountable.

It is the elected legislatures, whose members are so anxious to become part of the executive elite, that have abandoned their constitutional responsibility to hold the executive to account. It is the elected legislative branch of government that must be reformed if we are ever to return to anything even remotely resembling responsible government. The executive will not make it easy.

It will require strong commitment and intestinal fortitude from those with legislative authority if they are ever to rescue parliamentary supremacy from an executive government intent on its demise.

15.

ELECTORAL REFORM, REPRESENTATIVE RECALL, AND CITIZENS' INITIATIVES

The subject of citizen engagement and empowerment is a complex one and I approach it with some trepidation, especially regarding the topic of electoral reform. I am not an expert on electoral reform; others are and have written extensively on the subject. I encourage you to consult published studies of comparative electoral models. They are many and varied.[1]

Moreover, I am a recent, and admittedly reluctant, convert to the school of electoral reform. Although I concede that the first past the post (FPTP) system results in bizarre mathematical distortions, I continue to believe generally that how a legislature functions is much more relevant to responsible government than how it is chosen.

I am skeptical, too, of proportional representation (PR), especially in the purest forms, because it emphasizes entirely voting for a party as opposed to voting for an individual. In a pure PR system, there are simply lists provided by the parties. If your party gets 10 percent of the votes, you elect 10 percent of the members. However, this system precludes any prospect of an independent getting elected, does not provide for any elected member to serve any specific electoral district, and places even more authority in the party establishment, who prepare the lists and rank their preferred candidates at the top of that list.

FPTP works well in elections where there are only two competitive parties, such as in the United States. However, in places with a more diverse slate of political parties, the system breaks down. In Canada, a third or fourth party that polled 10 percent nationally, evenly distributed, would elect no members under FPTP; as opposed to 10 percent of the members or 31 MPs under proportional representation.

FPTP admittedly results in manufactured majorities. In the last federal elections, the Conservatives captured 39 percent of the vote, which translated into 60 percent of the seats and 100 percent of the power.

There are other concerning mathematical distortions under FPTP. I represent approximately 150,000 citizens in the electoral district of Edmonton-St. Albert. In Prince Edward Island, the average riding is closer to 40,000 people, meaning that a citizen of Prince Edward Island's vote is worth 3.5 times what the vote of an Albertan is worth. The disparity is even greater in the more sparsely populated ridings of the northern territories, a fact that compromises the democratic equality of all Canadian citizens.

The final distortion concerning FPTP is the efficacy of voting. In single-member constituencies, any votes for the winning candidate in excess of the votes for candidate finishing second (the notional "post") are wasted. Similarly, any votes not cast in favour of the winning candidate are similarly wasted in the winner take all system. Vote splitting and strategic voting become realities when sophisticated voters are mindful that their vote is likely to be wasted (as for example, by voting Green in Alberta for example).

I was the victim of vote splitting in the 2004 provincial election. There were four parties represented on the ballot, but only two candidates in realistic contention — myself, the incumbent, and the eventual winner, David Eggen from the NDP. However, a new conservative party, the Alberta Alliance, which would one day merge and morph into the Wildrose Party, contested its first election in 2004. They were a fledging party and not even remotely competitive in Edmonton; however, their non-campaigning candidate's 513 votes were arguably responsible for my 337 vote defeat. I remain convinced that had the fourth party not been on the ballot, I would have won that election in Edmonton-Calder, but such are the distortions inherent in the first past the post system.

The merits of the other electoral systems that exist, combined with my defeat in 2004, eventually interested me in a system of preferential voting frequently used in nomination and party leadership contests. To save the time needed for successive rounds of voting, electors rank their choices. If no candidate receives 50 percent + 1 on the first ballot, the last place candidate's second preferences are then added to the number of votes received by the other candidates and this process is repeated until one candidate has a clear majority.

I believe that under this system I would have been successful in 2004. Eggen won with just over 40 percent support and the Alberta Alliance candidate finished last (fourth). I believe most, if not all, of those 512 electors would have ranked me second; and those second preferences would have vaulted me over the NDP and above the magical 50 percent requirement.

But the electoral system obviously cannot be designed to remedy a defeated candidate's understanding as to what factors caused him to lose. The more relevant question is: Would more electors in Edmonton-Calder have preferred to be represented by a small "c" conservative, regardless of which party banner they were running under?

My left-leaning sister, who lives in British Columbia, is concerned about exactly this type of vote splitting, albeit on the left, between the Greens and the NDP, which she believes contributed to the re-election of Christy Clark's Liberals in 2013. Her solution is a version of the preferential ballot, where the voter would first make a choice between left (Green/NDP) and the B.C. right (Liberal/Conservative) and then choose which party the voter actually prefers within his or her broad choice.

As a social scientist, she believes this methodology would reduce strategic voting and vote splitting; apparently she wanted to vote Green, but voted NDP in the hope that a Liberal incumbent would be defeated.

However, in my view all her proposed system does is create a preferential ballot with a presumed preference. It presumes that a Green voter's second choice would be NDP and vice versa. I am not convinced that is a valid presumption. I suspect many Liberal's second choice might actually be NDP and vice versa. So, perhaps there should be a third voting matrix called "Centre." Or, better yet, the system should allow the voter to determine his or her own second preference, rather than attempting to presume it in advance.

Other attempts at ensuring elected legislatures are more representative of the governed have evolved. Some version of one of these systems would certainly be appealing since federal-ly, over half, and sometimes as many as two-thirds, of our MPs are elected on a plurality, rather than by a majority, of the votes cast in their electoral districts.

List proportional representation electoral systems are popular in Europe and attempt to apportion a party's seat share to its vote share. In its purest form, no single member is responsible for any particular constituency, as all are elected from preferential lists determined by the national parties. South Africa uses such a system, which in my view places even more importance on the party at the expense of personal representation. In such a system, there is no role for independent candidates, as all legislators are elected based on their party affiliation.

A variation, and more acceptable version, of this is the mixed-member proportional system (MMPV) used in Germany since the end of the Second World War, and more recently in New Zealand. Between half and two-thirds of the seats are elected in single-member constituencies under FPTP. The remaining seats are "assigned" to parties to compensate for any disproportionality produced by the FPTP voting.

A further, more complicated, version of this, rejected by B.C. voters, is the single transferable vote (STV), which employs multi-seat districts. In this system, electors rank candidates, either from a list prepared by the parties or from one including candidated from across party lines. To be elected, a candidate must surpass a specified quota. Thereafter, voter preferences are reallocated until the previously excluded candidates receive the quota. The system, used in Ireland and Northern Ireland, is repeated until all of the seats are filled. STV would allow independents to be competitive, but its complication is its largest drawback. Given already waning voter turnout, I cannot promote a system whose complication would further discourage voter participation.

A final system, similar to the preferential system described above, is the alternative vote (AV) used in Australia. AV uses single-seat districts and voters rank their preference. If no candidate receives a majority based on the first preferences, second preferences from the last-place candidate are considered until a majority is obtained. This "preferential" system is frequently used in party nominations and even leadership contests. AV ensures the successful local candidate receives an eventual majority of support from his or her constituents, but it does not necessarily reduce party disparities. Indeed, in many instances it would exacerbate them. For example, if 40 percent of the election is left-leaning (NDP/Green) and 60 percent is centre-right (Lib/Con), AV could easily wipe out the NDP and the Greens, where invariably they would elect members under either FPTP or PR.

All systems have strengths, pitfalls, and the possibility for distortions. FPTP leads to strong governments and therefore stability. However, this leads to centrally controlled decision making behind closed doors. Alternative systems increase the prospect of coalitions and therefore the need for co-operation and collaboration between parliamentarians. Most democracies employ voting systems under which majorities are earned, not manufactured as they are under FPTP. Governments that depend upon multi-party support will, by necessity, be more open and inclusive. The result is more transparent governing and less behind-closed-door brokering.

For what it is worth, I prefer MMPV over PR or STV. The latter two systems sacrifice local representation in order to gain party proportionality. As a critic of too much party control, I believe that that is not a positive trade-off.

I believe that functional democracy is premised on effective representation. Party discipline, which has evolved into partisan wrangling and control from the centre, is contrary to effective representation. Party platforms transform MPs into delegates of that platform rather than true representatives who will study the issues individually and then cast an intelligent vote thereafter. Names of political parties did not even appear on the ballot in Canada until 1972. In my view, for Canadian democracy to heal itself, we must once again focus more on the strength of the individual representatives in Parliament and less on the spin and marketing of the party.

An electoral system that encourages diverse perspectives will require governments to consider and navigate that political diversity. Such a system will not only be more democratic, but will also lead to better long-term governance. At present, unnecessarily rigid party discipline is destroying representative democracy. Many of the alternatives to our system, such as proportional representation and other electoral variations only serve to solidify the concept of party over constituency.

In my view, it matters less how a representative is selected than how he or she performs once elected. For citizens to be empowered, they need to be more concerned with electing an individual to serve as their representative. For responsible government to work, governments must be responsible to the legislatures, leaders accountable to their caucuses, and representatives answerable to their constituents.

For the latter to take place, it is necessary that, if the electors in an electoral district are sufficiently displeased with their representative, they should be entitled to fire or "recall" him or her.

British Columbians accepted such a novel democratic concept (along with the citizen initiative, to be discussed shortly) in a 1991 referendum.[2] The process is commenced by a petition. The petitioner must reside in the electoral district of the member to be recalled. If the quota of electors demanding recall (a high 40 percent in British Columbia) is obtained within the sixty day collection period, the Speaker of the Legislature announces the seat has been vacated and a by-election is called. The recalled MLA can contest the by-election if she believes she still has the support of her constituency, and can thus confirm she has a continuing mandate. The legislation has never successfully recalled a member, although in 1998 Paul Reitsma, who had been implicated in a scandal in which he was accused of using assumed names to write letters to the editors of various newspapers praising of his own talents, resigned his seat in the B.C. Legislature, when recall appeared imminent.

I support recall legislation, although I believe the threshold in British Columbia is unnecessarily high. Achieving the support of 40 percent of the electorate for a recall petition seems unlikely given that in provincial elections voter turnout of 50 percent is becoming acceptable.

In a democracy, sovereignty derives from the citizenry and it is that electorate that has exclusive legal standing to complain when a member has done wrong by them. When a member is involved in some scandal or crosses the floor to change parties or simply quits a party, as when I resigned from the Conservative caucus to sit as an independent, the inevitable chirping starts, from the ditched party, and sometimes from the media, that the member should resign and submit to a by-election to verify continued support in the community that elected him. But in a democracy, neither one's political opponents nor the media get to determine a who serves as the people's representative; that right is reserved for the electorate. Recall legislation would give the constituents affected the exclusive right, between elections, to determine who is to represent them and in the process significantly improve representative democracy.

❖

Apart from the power to recall their representatives, there are other options for citizen empowerment, such tenets of direct democracy as the plebiscite and citizen's initiative, that need to be considered. Again, others, such as Patrick Boyer, have canvassed these topics extensively and I encourage you to consult those thorough texts.[3,4]

Although I support direct democracy conceptually, I am mindful of the limitations both constitutional and practical that exist with it. Accordingly, I disagree with those who believe that citizen's initiatives and referenda are panaceas for a broken Canadian democracy.

The practical realities of direct democracy are quite simple. The desires of the majority would be in perpetual conflict. For example, consider two questions that might appear on a ballot: Do you support more free medical care? And do you want lower taxes? Certainly, both questions would be answered overwhelmingly in the positive. But they cannot co-exist, at least not without taking away some other public good.

The other practical limitation of the plebiscite is the inevitable involvement of special interest groups. As an illustration, Edmontonians voted to keep its City Centre Airport open in 1992. However, a well-organized lobby group of property developers, eager to get their hands on the valuable downtown land, were able to get the requisite signatures to put the question on the ballot a second time. The massive advertising campaign financed by the property development lobby could not be matched by the flying clubs and small charter companies that operated out of the "muni." The pro-closure lobby outspent the pro-muni forces 4:1 in that plebiscite and won decisively. The airport closed ten years later, but the issue remains unresolved and the subject of ongoing litigation. The airport was popular and arguably supported by a majority of the citizens. But the deep pockets of the closure side were able to advertise its way to victory.

The constitutional limitations of direct democracy are slightly more complicated.

In British Columbia, the requisite number to put a question to the people is 10 percent of the voters in every single constituency. Bill Vander Zalm was able to collect the requisite signatures for his campaign to get rid of the Harmonized Sales Tax (HST), and in 2011, British Columbians voted to abolish it.

The Constitution Act gives exclusive law-making authority to Parliament over matters assigned to it pursuant to section 91. Similarly, section 92 gives exclusive law-making authority to the provincial legislature regarding matters assigned thereafter. Although it is generally agreed that Parliament or a provincial legislature can delegate a question for ratification to the electorate, it is a matter of some academic and legal dispute whether Parliament can be bound by a decision that originated in a plebiscite.

Such a concern was raised by the Judicial Committee of the Privy Council (then the final court of appeal in Canada) in 1914. Lord Howell opined that a law not supported by the Crown could not stand and therefore Crown assent was required. "Who is to be responsible for the legislation ... if there is no representative of the people promoting the legislation?" the jurist queried.[5]

No comparable argument can be made concerning the constitutionality of ratification by referendum of a decision made by Parliament or a legislature. Accordingly, I see an important and specific role for direct democracy in ratification of constitutional amendments, as was unsuccessfully tried regarding the Charlottetown Accord in 1993. Given that a constitution is the social contract between the citizen and the state, it is most appropriate that amendments to it be ratified by those affected.

I see value in direct democracy and electoral reform, but I am less enthusiastic about their ability to remedy democratic deficits than other commentators. I prefer representative democracy, and, accordingly, I enthusiastically embrace workable recall legislation.

Admittedly, the fact that citizens are craving more direct democracy is evidence that they are dissatisfied with how their democratic institutions are currently performing. However, I believe that a system with elected officials charged with studying legislative proposals and providing financial oversight is generally a better system than what is achievable via direct democracy, given its limitations and potential for undue influence by special interests. A legislature properly empowered, comprised of members accountable to their electorate is the key to effective representation and responsible government.

16. —231

DEMOCRATIC REFORM: THE OPPOSITION MANTRA

The ideas in this book are not new. Many good books, essays, and op-ed columns have been written detailing the myriad and ever increasing democratic deficits in Canada. In fact, when I recently re-read parts of Preston Manning's excellent 1992 treatise *The New Canada*,[1] I was reminded that I am not the only politician who has felt both constricted and ineffective inside the parliamentary system, and powerless to change it.

Being a backbench MP in a majority government caucus is, without a doubt, the worst job in Canadian politics. Whereas Opposition members can stand upon a soapbox and decry the government's shoddy performance on the issue *du jour*, and cabinet ministers are, at the very least, close enough to the levers of power that they can communicate with them, a government backbencher's role is limited to cheerleading and barking on command.

Manning understood this intuitively. "Party discipline forces them [MPs] to vote against their constituents' wishes on matters of fundamental importance … straining … the trust that made their election to Parliament possible in the first place."[2]

The Reform Movement and Party, which Manning helped found and then led, was dedicated largely, but not exclusively, to democratic reform. It believed in a Triple-E Senate (elected, equal, and effective). The Reform Party's 1991 statement of principles further promoted free and fair elections, direct democracy, including the use of citizens' initiatives and referenda, and, most notably, a representative Parliament, where elected members had a duty to their constituents that "should supersede their obligations to their political parties."

Wow! Can you believe that Stephen Harper once belonged to a Reform caucus that advocated loyalty to something other than to the political party?

Manning talked openly about breaking up the tyranny of the present-day Family Compact (bureaucrats, politicians, and special interests), and promised a democratic caucus in which positions "will be adopted by majority decision after open debate without heavy-handed direction from the party leadership."[3] How disappointed Manning must be in his prodigy! Of course, the current prime minister subscribed to economic reform more than he believed in democratic reform.

The Reform Party never won more than sixty seats under Manning's leadership, and a lack of party discipline, especially regarding social conservative members and candidates, is often cited as the reason for the party's limited electoral success. Manning admitted that Reform's populism had the unintended effect of attracting people with intolerant views. I believe that it is undeniable that the perception of Reform as being intolerant of minorities and homophobic prevented it from catching on in mainstream Central Canada.

These early lessons were not lost on Stephen Harper or his handlers. Harper's electoral success has been incremental and commensurate with his ability to shed his, and the reborn Conservative Party's, "scary" image. The party won 99 seats in 2004, 124 in 2006, 143 in 2008, and a majority of 166 in 2011. Increased message control (e.g., talking points) and party discipline (e.g., the lack of reluctance to throw candidates who go off-side under the bus) are undoubtedly responsible for Harper's increased electoral success.

Another modern-day democratic reformer, Danielle Smith of the Alberta Wildrose, showed much less appetite for firing off-side candidates; and it likely cost her Wildrose the 2012 provincial election. Two urban candidates, running in ridings where Wildrose was barely competitive, had expressed homophobic and racist views late in the campaign. There was internal pressure for Ms. Smith to fire the candidates, who were unlikely to win their constituencies anyway. But to her credit (sort of), she defended both freedom of speech and her candidates. The electoral calculation was, however, fatal, and Ms. Smith now acknowledges the need to vet candidates to ensure that no one is nominated who cannot express his views "respectfully."

I have great respect for Danielle Smith, and Wildrose represents many of the same views, and has many of the same people, as the original Reform Party. Wildrose has a democratic reform menu that includes fixed election dates and an official policy of allowing more free votes in the Alberta Legislature. In fact, according the 2012 Wildrose policy manual, all votes in the legislature and in caucus should be free and transparently reported to the public. Motions of non-confidence would remain, but would be stand-alone and presumably declared. The party also supports an elected, accountable Senate for Canada and would introduce legislation allowing for citizen-initiated referenda and to the recall of MLAs by disappointed electors. These critical initiatives would genuinely improve Alberta's democracy, which has seen voter turnout as low as 41 percent in the last six years.

However, will any of it ever come to pass? Much of Wildrose's democratic reform playbook could have been lifted from Preston Manning's *The New Canada*. However, Reform morphed into the Canadian Alliance, which merged with the Progressive Conservatives to form the Conservative Party of Canada. There are still four MPs from the original class of '93, including the prime minister. Yet the entirety of Reform's democratic reform mantra has disappeared, sacrificed to the altar of electoral expediency, save for a remaining vague commitment to Senate reform. Although the CPC policy manual still calls for an elected Senate, Prime Minister Harper has appointed over half of the current unelected senators, including eighteen in one day.

Most pundits believe the Harper government to be the most secretive, controlled, and tightly scripted government in Canadian history. If Wildrose ever wins power in Alberta, will they be any truer to their commitment to democratic reform? Or is democratic reform incompatible with governing and therefore the exclusive rallying cry for opposition parties and advocacy groups? I am hoping for the former, but fear it might be the latter. It must be noted that in 2013 the Wildrose leader took no time distancing herself and her party from her former campaign manager, Tom Flannagan, after he made comments, which arguably were taken out of context, but seemed to support the viewing of child pornography. Perhaps freedom of opinion is incompatible with electoral success.

Although democratic reform is undoubtedly a vote-getter, it is far from a major vote-getter. To some extent, it is largely "inside baseball," a preoccupation of journalists, some academics, and disaffected politicians such as me. Most voters are more concerned with pocketbook issues than with how dysfunctional the capital is. Nor am I convinced that any voter is particularly concerned about a lack of job satisfaction experienced by backbench MPs.

Accordingly, promises of tax cuts and lower cellphone bills will invariably attract more voters than undeliverable promises of an elected Senate or more free votes in Parliament. By the same logic, a government can abandon its commitment to democratic reform once elected with impunity if, in so doing, it finds less resistance in delivering its promises of tax cuts and lower phone bills.

However, as this book has hopefully demonstrated, irresponsible government (which is a government that is not accountable to the elected assembly) has not served Canadians well. The effect of decades of the devolution of the supremacy of Parliament has been over $600 billion of debt at the federal level alone ($1.2 trillion of all Canadian governments at all levels). Somebody is going to have to pay that money back some day; in the meantime, debt-servicing charges will continue to limit governments' spending ability and distort their taxation policies.

For Canadians to buy into democratic reform *en masse* and for politicians therefore to maintain a commitment to reform ideals once they are in a position to deliver on them, the electorate will need to be convinced that reform is in their best interest in a tangible way, not merely at a conceptual level.

Change is also going to take extraordinary leaders, men and women with unshakeable values and belief in democratic reform, leaders who will not shake or cower at the first sign of softening poll numbers or a bureaucracy resistant to reform. It will require leadership committed to the long game, who realize that the devolution of parliamentary institutions took a half-century to occur, and that it may take that long to restore them. Like the destruction of responsible government, the rebuilding of it will, by necessity, occur in incremental baby steps. There is no magic bullet to save our failing democracy, and even if there was, the current power structure would prevent it from being deployed. But there are a plethora of smaller reforms that will someday allow for major reform. We will canvass these in the concluding chapter.

17. · 244 📝 Fix.

CONCLUSIONS:
WHERE DO WE GO FROM HERE?

Canada has had responsible government since 1848, and a Constitution since 1867. The latter remains substantially unaltered; the former has been almost completely destroyed. The checks and balances designed in the constitutional documents and conventions on which this country is based have broken down to the degree that executive power is nearly absolute. Parliament's ability to perform its role of government oversight has declined to the point that it is entirely ineffective.

When Canada was founded in 1867, its system of governing was appropriate for the day. Canada was a large, sparsely populated country, one that seemed difficult to hold together. Our neighbours to the south had just been immersed in a bloody Civil War and our Fathers of Confederation were openly skeptical of too much democracy and rampant republicanism. Accordingly, they designed a system that maintained a concentration of power at the centre but made the executive accountable to a democratically elected assembly. At the heart of our system of government is a bicameral Parliament, but the upper house is an appointed one, chosen by the executive branch, not an elected one, as is the case in the United States.

Although suitable for the era in which it was created, our system of government contained within it the seeds for the devolution of responsible democratic government. To make matters worse, the country's inability to design a workable constitutional amending formula (both before and after 1982) has made remedying the democratic deficits and reversing the devolution impracticable.

Given that maintenance of the status quo favours those who exercise executive power, it is perhaps not surprising that a new Family Compact comprised of politicians, bureaucrats, and special interests has evolved. In substance, the new Family Compact was, and is, not dissimilar to the one William Lyon Mackenzie rallied against in 1837. Moreover, the current elected Parliament is more consultative than supreme, not dissimilar to the one Mackenzie served in.

❖

Virtually all countries have some form of a democracy and democratic assembly. Even Iran has the 290-member Islamic Consultative Assembly, with members elected to four year terms. The body is appropriately named as consultative. Real power rests with the Supreme Leader, who is chosen by a committee of clerics styled the Assembly of Experts.

Similarly, China has an elected National People's Congress. However, this is a rubber-stamp legislature. Power rests with the Communist Party of China (CPC, ironically). In fact, it is written into China's constitution that the general secretary of the Communist Party of China is also China's president.

As the previous chapters have demonstrated, Canada's elected assemblies have increasingly become rubber-stamping bodies or assemblies of consultation only, and as the previous chapters have also demonstrated real power is increasingly concentrated in the executive. I do not wish to draw too close a comparison between Canada and the above mentioned authoritarian states, but I do wish to point out that the struggle for democracy, at its core, involves finding an appropriate balance between the legislative and executive branches.

The test by which we may measure a country's promotion of freedom and democracy is the role, power, and efficacy of the elected legislative branch. Is the legislature a meaningful check on executive power or is it purely consultative? Does the elected assembly actually hold the government to account or is it merely ceremonial? Does Parliament provide effective oversight or is it ornamental?

I admire some aspects of the American system, with its formal separation of powers. The U.S. Congress is a powerful institution with real legislative and oversight powers. Leaders of Senate committees are real power brokers and testifying before a congressional committee can be an intimidating and even frightening experience (just ask Roger Clemens or Mark McGwire)![1] The U.S. Congress serves as a functional check on the executive power of the Office of the President. Some have suggested that it is perhaps too effective, disputes between the U.S. president and Congress frequently can, and recently has, lead to gridlock, where nothing gets done. Such disputes have even resulted in the shutdown of the entire U.S. federal government.

Canada, on the other hand, has too few checks and balances, which allows for a near complete concentration of power within the Prime Minister's Office. The lack of checks and balances within the Canadian system allows PMO staffers to control parliamentarians, Parliament, and even House and Senate committees.

The most notorious example of the abuse of unchecked executive power in Canada's Parliament occurred when PMO operatives intervened in a Senate audit committee by reimbursing the inappropriately claimed funds and then attempted to sanitize the audit report. The prime minister claims to have not been apprised of this chicanery, demonstrating, if nothing else, that the unelected staffers within the PMO are accountable to no one, not even the prime minister.

To avoid a repeat of such misdeeds, we need to design a system with fewer checks and balances than the American system, thus avoiding the likelihood of gridlock, but more checks and balances than the Canadian, thus avoiding the reality of unaccountable and irresponsible government.

Rebalancing power will be incremental just as the demise of democracy has been.

Michael Chong's reform bill is a good start. This legislation will begin to rebalance the power dynamic between party leaders and their caucuses. If passed, it will remove the requirement that a party leader endorse a candidate for election under that party banner. This has been used to give the leader a veto over decisions of local riding associations that have held a local nomination. This fundamentally alters the relationship between caucus and leader. Currently, the caucus member is much less likely to challenge the leader, making the leader the master over the caucus, not accountable to it. This change will help restore democracy by making the candidate, and eventual parliamentarian, accountable to his or her constituents not the servant of the leader.

Secondly, the Reform Act[2] will allow the caucus to trigger a leadership review based on a petition of 20 percent of the caucus and a majority vote by secret ballot thereafter. This again makes the leader accountable to the elected caucus rather than to an inflated membership, which never meets and in fact no longer exists after the leader has been selected.

Finally, Chong's reforms will allow the caucus to elect their chairs and admit or eject members based on the same 20/50 percent rules. These are all currently exclusive prerogatives of the leader thus cementing his or her control over the caucus.

These changes, if passed, will re-establish the leader's role as a leader, rather than a lord, over the caucus.

Another initiative currently before Parliament might someday allow committees of the House of Commons to elect their own chairs, rather than having them appointed by the Prime Minister's Office (or Opposition Leader's Office). This would be an improvement over the current system, where paid chairmanships are doled out to loyal partisans, who are removed if they dare challenge or disappoint their leadership.[3]

An obvious and logical extension of this concept would be to formalize and make permanent the committee membership at the beginning of a Parliament (or at the very least at the beginning of a parliamentary session). Security of tenure would allow committee members to take their job of vetting, as opposed to cheerleading for, government legislation seriously.

This would greatly improve the current system, where committee members hold their positions at the pleasure of their respective leaders and can easily be removed or substituted. I am all too familiar with how both of these tactics can be used by the government for its own purposes.

I was removed from the Public Safety Committee and transferred to the Library of Parliament Committee after questioning $16 orange juice and other cabinet minister opulence. Members of Parliament should not be punished for doing their jobs. Nor should committee members currently be substituted for a specified tactical exercise. This famously occurred on June 5, 2013, when members of the Access and Privacy Committee, who supported my public servant salary disclosure bill, were subbed out in favour of members attempting to gain favour within the Prime Minister's Office.

❖

Bolstering the functioning of the Speaker would also help to improve the functioning of Parliament and, by extension, the health of democracy in Canada. The Speaker is the presiding authority over the House of Commons. That is not something to boast of, as, currently, the House of Commons functions with dysfunction. Decorum is poor and important procedural matters, such as time allocation, are determined by simple majority, thus allowing the tyranny of the majority to suppress parliamentary debate and oversight.

The Speaker's authority must be increased and the method of selection changed. Currently, the Speaker is chosen at the commencement of a Parliament by the members via a secret ballot. Being elected, and certainly being re-elected by a subsequent Parliament, requires the maintenance of collegial relations with the members. This, arguably, is inconsistent with a role that requires one to maintain order and make rulings that do not favour any particular side or individual(s).

Being a successful trial judge or hockey referee is in no way dependent upon being popular among lawyers or players. In fact, a cogent argument can be made that to be a good in either of those roles it is necessary to be the exact opposite, i.e., unpopular — at least some of the time. Not only is it necessary for the Speaker to maintain a certain amount of popularity, the Speaker must, initially at least, be partisan, since to be elected as Speaker it is necessary, first, to be elected as a Member of Parliament under a specific party banner. Although overt bias has certainly not been present under the two speakers that I have served under, true objectivity and respect amongst both MPs and the public should involve removal of even the apprehension or potential for bias.[4]

The system worked better when incumbent speakers ran unopposed in subsequent general elections. Essentially, a Speaker, once elected, had the respect of all parties, who would, thereafter, ensure his re-election, thus removing any requirement that the Speaker be partisan or even popular in order to ensure re-election to the prestigious chair.

But I am not sure that the Speaker needs to be elected by his peers or even needs be a member. Arguably, having an effective presiding officer with no connection to any party or any individual members would be preferable to the present system. A superior court judge or esteemed academic chancellor could become an officer of Parliament and provide objective and arbitrary, but fair, referee services to the increasingly dysfunctional House proceedings. Thereafter, the powers of the Speakers must be enhanced to ensure fairness in parliamentary process and adequate vetting of government legislation.

The current government's two favourite abuses of parliamentary processes are restricted time allocations and omnibus bills. Use of the former allows a majority government to limit debate on its own terms and at its own discretion, as it is accomplished by simple majority motion. The latter forces the opposition to vote on a bundle of often disjointed and unrelated pieces of legislation, thereby denying the Opposition the opportunity to give individual scrutiny to each piece.

Time allocation and closure should only be granted at the discretion of the Speaker, or by the unanimous consent of the House. If an air traffic control strike is threatening air safety, back-to-work legislation is required urgently enough to necessitate an expedited debate and vote. But this should be the exception and not the norm. Arguably, no comparable emergency existed to pass the Canada-Honduras Free Trade Agreement, for example.[5]

The standing orders currently allow the Speaker to assess applications for emergency debates. The Speaker will permit an emergency debate when the matter is urgent and cannot be dealt with through normal channels or parliamentary processes. This system works exceptionally well and a similar discretion ought to be vested within the Speaker to determine when a situation justifies time allocation or closure.

Although the Speaker has limited authority to order separate votes on unrelated portions contained inside omnibus bills, that discretion is used infrequently. Moreover, ordering separate votes does nothing to promote a separate debate on an issue unrelated to the rest of the omnibus package. Just as there is a requirement for "issue disjoinder" in civil litigation, there should be a requirement to break up omnibus bills into digestible pieces of related legislation. It is indefensible to put an amendment to the Supreme Court Act, allowing for federal court judges who once practised law in Quebec to be appointed as a Quebec judge to the Supreme Court, inside a budget implementation act. The standing orders need to be amended to prohibit this abusive practice and afford Speaker the power to enforce the rules of procedural fairness.

An unbelievable event occurred in the House in March of 2014, when the House entertained an application to hold Conservative member Brad Butt in contempt of Parliament. Butt admitted to having been mistaken when he told the House that he had personally witnessed individuals retrieving discarded Elections Canada voter cards and then using them to go vote. This false witness was offered to support the government's attempt, through the Fair Elections Act, to decrease the incidence of voter fraud.

The Speaker found a *prima facie* case of contempt for deliberately misleading Parliament. But a majority of the House (all CPC members) was able to defeat a motion to refer the matter to committee, thereby killing it. Clearly, the presiding officer must be able to deal with matters of contempt, not have them decided by a partisan majority.

❖

A similar procedural threat to democracy occurs frequently in the House committee system, when a member moves to move a matter in camera and the non-debateable motion is thereafter determined by simple majority motion. There are obvious times when a committee must go in camera, such as when matters of national security are under consideration. However, the current government will move a matter into private discussion for the simple reason that it prefers to discuss a politically complicated matter without the prying eyes of the media. This is a blatant example of abuse of procedure to avoid accountability; moving in camera must be restricted to situations requiring witness protection, not those situations where the government requires cover.

Applications to go in camera should be determined by the chair, according to predetermined criteria, not by the simple majority vote of a committee doing the government's heavy lifting and taking their direction from the Prime Minister's Office. Decisions of committee chairs should be subject to an appeal to the Speaker but immune from challenges by the members, as occurs currently. At present, challenges to the chair occur because the majority did not like the ruling and wish to have it overturned, not because there has been an improper ruling or procedural irregularity. Challenging a chair is normally a serious matter, calling into question the chair's ability, neutrality, and integrity. The process must be prohibited when it is used merely because a majority of the members are of a different political party than the chair and are opposed to the ruling.

Security of tenure, for both committee chairs and a Speaker with significantly enhanced authority, will promote fairness in their rulings and remove criticisms of partisan bias, which is especially prevalent at the House committee level.

❖

Modifications to our electoral system may further improve our democracy. In theory, proportional representation, or some variation, will lead to coalition governments rather than "manufactured" majority governments. This has the potential to force co-operation and collaboration rather than authoritarian "adversarialism." However, coalition governments will frequently be financially reckless, as coalition partners bring their expensive demands to the table as a condition for continued support.

Greater citizen participation, through direct democracy, will also improve some aspects of our democratic deficit. Although there are constitutional limitations on citizens' initiative legislation (such as a demand binding the Crown to spend money it does not have), approval of already passed legislation by citizen-initiated referenda will serve as a useful check on legislative power. Moreover, citizens must have the right to recall their Member of Parliament or member of the Legislative Assembly based on significant popular disapproval of his or her performance. Updated access to information laws will give citizens the information we require to allow for greater informed participation.

Citizens maintaining a check on their legislatures and legislators will advance a system where those legislatures provide an effective check on the executive and first ministers. Finally, whistle-blower protection that actually protects whistle-blowers, not government, and a media dedicated to informed debate will all contribute to restoring confidence in a better functioning democracy.

❖

Generally, I believe that the Westminster system of parliamentary democracy can be made to work. I believe that responsible government, where the executive, through the cabinet, is responsible to the legislative branch is preferable to the U.S. congressional system, with its formal separation of powers. The elected Parliament is the centrepiece of democracy and its elected members must take their role as legislators seriously. They must be earnest in their role in providing financial oversight and holding government to account. Members of Parliament must have the authority and autonomy to act on behalf of their constituents, as opposed to shilling for their party leadership, for the system to work.

Loyalty to constituency must take precedence over loyalty to party and party leadership. Caucus members must be able to vote freely, except in obvious matters of confidence such as the budget and the main estimates. However, the estimates must be subject to actual scrutiny not rubber-stamping or "deemed" approval. Modifications ought to be able to be made by Parliament to ensure proper oversight. And once the line items have all been approved, and/or modified and approved, the entire estimates package, by necessity, must be treated as a matter of confidence.

Matters on which the party specifically campaigned in the previous election can properly be whipped by party leadership. Specific items in an electoral platform all form part of a social contract between the voters and their representatives. But these matters must have been specifically campaigned on. A vague platform of safe streets and safe communities, for example, cannot be used to compel a member thereafter to support an aggressive minimum mandatory sentence for a specified crime.

True and actual government members (the prime minister, the cabinet, and, by extension, parliamentary secretaries) will continue to take a position and vote as a block on government bills and motions. But backbenchers (and Opposition MPs) should never be similarly bound. Moreover, private members' business and Opposition bills and motions should never be whipped. The government controls so much of the parliamentary calendar as it is; if it wants to make something a government priority, it has every opportunity to do so. The fact that a government has not done so demonstrates that the subject matter is not a key government initiative and, therefore, private members ought to be able to raise the matter and have it determined by a free vote of all of the members.

No backbench member of any caucus should ever face any discipline for exercising his or her right to vote freely, subject to the above limited exceptions. No MP should be disciplined for doing her job and representing her constituents. Party leadership must use cogent argument and logical suasion to gain support of their caucus, not discipline and threat of expulsion.

Members of Parliament must become something other, something more, than aspiring members of the executive cabinet. Similar to being a member of the U.S. Congress, being a legislator should be an important end in itself, not merely the means to a perceived higher end — being asked to join to the executive cabinet.

This is going to require a fundamental shift in how we view parliamentarians. Being a democratically elected legislator must be given the respect it deserves. Media should no longer refer to long-tenured parliamentarians as "career backbenchers." Nobody ever referred to Ted Kennedy's near half-century in the U.S. Senate with derision or disrespect!

Perhaps if parliamentarians began to take themselves more seriously in their role of holding government to account the public and media would begin to take them more seriously. Empowerment should come from within the legislators themselves; Michael Chong's Reform Bill will assist in the process.

However, legislators will never take their critical role in holding government to account seriously so long as they consider themselves to be members of the executive in training.

Just as government backbenchers generally aspire to move to the middle and then eventually to the front benches, Opposition MPs, too, are interested in finding their way to the government front benches. Since this can only happen if their party defeats the governing party in an election, they are not for the most part dedicated to holding government to account either; they are dedicated only to embarrassing the government so that they can defeat it. Opposition members fancy themselves as the "government in waiting." Parliament will never function as an effective oversight body so long as all of its members aspire to be the part of some future executive.

Canada needs to develop a hybrid between its Westminster model, with a near complete concentration of power in the centre, and the U.S. congressional system, with its unworkable system of checks and balances leading to unsolvable gridlock.

When Lord Durham recommended responsible government for the United Colonies of Canada in 1840, I am not convinced he envisioned a cabinet comprised entirely of elected legislators. In Durham's day, the governor was appointed by London and the governor had discretion to appoint the executive council (cabinet). There is, and one must be mindful of, a conflict between those who spend taxpayers' money delivering government programs and those who pass the laws and approve the spending (and are supposed to be representing the taxpayers).

The U.S. Constitution acknowledges this conflict through the formal separation of executive and legislative power. Canada actually understood this until 1931, through the emolument convention, discussed in Chapter 6. Prior to 1931, Members of the House of Commons were prohibited from accepting a cabinet appointment unless they first resigned their seat and ran in a by-election. The rule was implemented, appropriately, by the pre-Confederation Independence of Parliament Act and served as a legislative assurance to reduce Crown influence in the colonial legislatures.

Eighty-five years after its repeal, we once again have a system where the executive has undue, or, more accurately, complete, influence in, and over, the legislative Parliament.

❖

In January 2014, I spoke at the "Freedom and Democracy" Conference in Taiwan. I met a legislator from Nauru, a new Pacific island republic of less than ten thousand citizens. He informed me that a system where the entirety of the cabinet was comprised of elected legislators was considered by his infant country, but it was ultimately rejected because it was feared that the executive would grow too powerful and would eventually dominate the legislature. Nauru feared inadequate checks and balances within such as system.

Accordingly, the Polynesian island opted for a modified or hybrid system, where only the first minister is a member of the Nauruan Parliament. His cabinet is generally (and ideally) chosen in a manner similar to U.S. cabinet secretaries, from outside of the legislative branch.

The German constitution is a variation of this model. The German chancellor is appointed after being elected by an absolute majority of the Bundestag, to which the chancellor and her government are politically accountable. The German government is dependent upon majority support in the House, a concept unique by European parliamentary standards but a workable hybrid between complete separation and complete fusion of power and function. But the chancellor is the only member of the government who can be held politically responsible by the Bundestag. Ministers need not be chosen from the German parliament, although the imperatives of coalition government means that ministers are increasingly chosen to appease coalition partners.

The chancellor can be removed by a vote of non-confidence by a majority of the members of the German parliament; the chancellor's ministers, however, are responsible to the chancellor, not the Bundestag, regardless of whether they are parliamentarians or appointed from outside.

Moreover, all parties in the Bundestag select their leadership (whips, chairs) by formal election within the Fraktion (caucus). Unlike the Westminster model, a German Fraktion whip or chair would never sit inside the cabinet.

Our system would greatly benefit from a greater separation of power between the executive and legislative branches like Germany, without a complete separation of powers like that in the United States. Responsible government and the confidence convention can be maintained, without Parliament devolving into a rubber-stamping body of cheerleaders and trained seals.

Parliamentarians would take their jobs more seriously if there was something in their political DNA besides a desire to be in government. Certainly, the first minister should be a parliamentarian and should answer for his government in Question Period. Moreover, he could serve as prime minister as long as, but only as long as, he held the confidence of the elected House.

The confidence convention, the critical aspect of responsible government, can be maintained.

But a first minister should not be able to manipulate support in the House by appointing grossly oversized cabinets, complimented by an equally unnecessary number of parliamentary secretaries. In the Canadian context, currently seventy members of a 160-member government caucus in a 308-seat Parliament have some executive designation. Moreover, the pure math cements party discipline. A loyally partisan MP's mathematical chance of promotion is better that one in two! Contrast that with Great Britain, where the House is twice as big and the cabinet twice as small; as a result, a British MP's chance of making cabinet is reduced to about one in thirty. With those odds, one is much more likely to take the important role of being a parliamentarian much more seriously. Further contrast this with the American system, where a Congressman or senator is constitutionally prohibited from serving as a cabinet secretary. As a result, the U.S. Congress is a serious law-making and oversight providing body.

In practice, U.S. presidents frequently cannot get sponsored legislation through Congress. That problem is not necessarily unique to systems with a complete separation of powers. In Great Britain, Margaret Thatcher's government lost twenty-two bills on the floor of the House of Commons. In the summer of 2013, David Cameron's coalition government lost an important vote on a motion to commit British soldiers to the increasingly hostile Syrian civil war.

However, these British government losses caused neither the fall of the government nor a constitutional crisis. The only result was that the British population, through its elected representatives, decided that it was not comfortable with another long, ostensibly unwinnable, war, and in Prime Minister Thatcher's case all defeated government legislation had to be withdrawn.

That is what parliamentary democracy looks like.

Canada would benefit greatly from a system where Parliament vets legislation and holds government to account. Canada would benefit from a system where the government is not so insecure and thin-skinned that it can neither accept constructive criticism nor tolerate the occasional loss on the floor of the House.

As any Olympic athlete knows, you never run, swim, or skate faster than when you are being pursued by another elite athlete. Government would benefit from a Parliament that challenged it and held its feet to the fire.

Even well-intentioned leaders must be subject to checks and balances. Holding governments to account vets bad legislation and improves good legislation. Holding them to account constantly challenges the government of the day to perform even better. Holding governments to account makes mediocre executives better, good cabinets great, and defeats bad governments.

Having a democratically elected chamber hold to account the appointed executive is the essence of responsible government and is fundamentally critical to both democratic accountability and to good governance. The government of Canada would greatly benefit from such a Parliament.

The road back to responsible government will be neither quick nor easy. But the fact that you have taken the time to read my thoughts gives me hope for our future. Thank you for interest in Canadian democracy!

NOTES

INTRODUCTION

1) "Residential Property Tax Estimator," City of Edmonton, accessed February 20, 2014, *http://coewebapps3.edmonton.ca/taxcalculator/default.aspx*.

2) Lorne Gunter, "Edmonton's debt doesn't add up," *Edmonton Sun*, July 25, 2013, *www.edmontonsun.com/2013/07/25/gunter-edmontons-debt-doesnt-add-up*.

3) Charles Lammam and Milagros Palacios, "Taxes versus the Necessities of Life: The Canadian Consumer Tax Index, 2013," *Fraser Alert*, April 2013, *www.fraserinstitute.org/uploaded-Files/fraser-ca/Content/research-news/research/publications/canadian-consumer-tax-index-2013.pdf*.

4) "Your Tax Dollar: 2011–2012 Fiscal Year," Department of Finance Canada, modified March 12, 2013, accessed November 8, 2013, *www.fin.gc.ca/tax-impot/2012/html-eng.asp*.

1. THE QUEST FOR RESPONSIBLE GOVERNMENT: FROM THE MAGNA CARTA TO LORD DURHAM

1) "Birth of the English Parliament: The First Parliaments," Parliament of the United Kingdom, accessed February 21, 2014, *www.parliament.uk/about/living-heritage/evolutionofparliament/originsofparliament/birthofparliament/overview/firstparliaments/*.

2) For a detailed analysis of the quest for responsible government, many great Canadian history texts offer excellent synopsises. My refresher course in Canadian history of the 1830s and 1840s was courtesy of: Will Ferguson, *Bastards & Boneheads* (Vancouver: Douglas & McIntyre, 1999).

3) As an interesting aside, the leader asked to form a government need not be the leader of the party with the most seats in the legislature. If no party has a clear majority of the seats, it is the leader with the support of the majority of all of the members who is likely to gain and maintain the confidence of the assembly.

2. PUBLIC DEBT: A RUNAWAY TRAIN WRECK

1) "Canada's Federal Debt," Canadian Taxpayer's Federation, accessed February 25, 2014, *www.debtclock.ca/*.

2) "Federal and Provincial net debt," Canadian Federation of Independent Business, accessed February 25, 2014, *www.cfib-fcei.ca/english/article/5428-federal-and-provincial-debt-clock.html*.

3) "Your Tax Dollar: 2011–2012 Fiscal Year," Department of Finance Canada, modified March 12, 2013, accessed November 8, 2013, *www.fin.gc.ca/tax-impot/2012/html-eng.asp*.

4) Ben Eisen, "Canada's public sector needs a trimming," *National Post*, June 7, 2011, *http://fullcomment.nationalpost.com/2011/06/07/ben-eisen-canadas-public-sector-needs-a-trimming/*.

5) "Canada's Federal Debt," Canadian Taxpayer's Federation, accessed February 25, 2014, *www.debtclock.ca/*.

6) Niels Veldhuis and Milagros Palacios,

"Mr. Flaherty, time to balance the budget," *Fraser Forum* (January/February 2013): 5–7, *http://issuu.com/fraserinstitute/docs/fraserforum_janfeb2013*.

7) Mark Milke, *Tax Me I'm Canadian: A Taxpayer's Guide to Your Money & How Politicians Spend It* (Kelowna, BC: Sandhill Book Marketing, 2013).

8) Ian Cowie, "Margaret Thatcher taught us more about money than any economist," *Telegraph*, April 8, 2013, *http://blogs.telegraph.co.uk/finance/ianmcowie/100023933/the-financial-wit-and-wisdom-of-baroness-thatcher/*.

9) Tasmin McMahon, "Why corporate welfare doesn't boost employment," *Maclean's*, February 6, 2014, *www2.macleans.ca/2014/02/06/toying-with-corporate-welfare/*.

10) Milke, *Tax Me*, 53.

11) Statistics Canada data compiled by Fraser Institute. Livio Di Matteo, *Measuring Canada in the Twenty-First Century: An International Overview of the Size and Efficiency of Government Spending* (Vancouver: Fraser Institute, 2014), 4, *www.fraserinstitute.org/research-news/display.aspx?id=20733*.

12) Canada, Parliament, House of Commons, "Chapter X: Financial Procedures," *Permanent and Provisional Standing Orders of the House of Commons,* January 2014, accessed February 25, 2014, *www.parl.gc.ca/About/House/StandingOrders/chap10-e.htm*.

13) Canada, Library of Parliament, Research Branch, *Reorganizing Government: New Approaches to Public Service Reform*, by Brian O'Neal, Ottawa: Library of Parliament, Research Branch, 1994, *http://publications.gc.ca/Collection-R/LoPBdP/BP/bp375-e.htm*.

14) Meagan Fitzpatrick, "Canada can't account for $3.1B in anti-terror funding, AG finds," CBC News, April 30, 2013, accessed February 25, 2014, *www.cbc.ca/news/politics/canada-can-t-account-for-3-1b-in-anti-terror-funding-ag-finds-1.1303999*.

15) Sophia Harris, "Canada Job Grant ads cost $2.5M for non-existent program," CBC News, January 14, 2014, accessed February 25, 2014, *www.cbc.ca/news/politics/canada-job-grant-ads-cost-2-5m-for-non-existent-program-1.2495196*.

16) Joan Bryden, "Tony Clement G8 Fund: New Documents Contradict Clement, Suggest He Carved Up $50-Million Fund," *Huffington Post*, November 23, 2011, accessed February 25, 2014, *www.huffingtonpost.ca/2011/11/23/tony-clement-g8-fund-documents_n_1109780.html*.

17) "Political Scandals: The Human Resources boondoggle," *The National*, February 7, 2000, accessed March 5, 2014, *www.cbc.ca/archives/categories/politics/federal-politics/scandals-boondoggles-and-white-elephants/the-human-resources-boondoggle.html*.

18) Canada, Parliament, House of Commons, "Business of Supply [Opposition Motion-Confidence in the Government]," *Debates*, 40th Parliament, 3rd Session, vol. 145, no. 149, March 25,

2011, *www.parl.gc.ca/HousePublica-tions/Publication.aspx?Language=E&-Mode=1&Parl=40&Ses=3&Do-cId=5072532.*

3. FEDERAL-PROVINCIAL COST SHARING: THERE IS ONLY ONE TAXPAYER

1) David Beatty, *Constitutional Law in Theory and Practice* (Toronto: University of Toronto Press, 1995), 47.
2) Canada, Library of Parliament, Research Branch, *National Standards and Social Programs: What the Federal Government Can Do*, by Jack Stillborn, Ottawa: Library of Parliament, Research Branch,1997, *www.parl.gc.ca/Content/LOP/Re-searchPublications/bp379-e.htm.*

4. PARLIAMENT: A BROKEN INSTITUTION

1) Peter Russell, quoted in Andrew Coyne, "Canada, like U.S., hostage to political minority," Canada.com, October 9, 2013, accessed March 5, 2014, *http://o.canada.com/news/canada-like-u-s-hostage-to-politi-cal-minority/.*
2) Josh Wingrove, "Former Tory whip slams party's decision to strip private member's bill," *Globe and Mail*, February 28, 2014, *www.theglobeandmail.com/news/politics/former-tory-whip-slams-partys-deci-sion-to-strip-private-members-bill/article17181042/.*
3) Budget Implementation Act (2012), Bill C-38, An Act to implement certain provisions of the budget tabled in Parliament on March 29, 2012 and other measures, as passed April 26, 2012 (Canada, 42nd Parl.,

1st sess.), *www.parl.gc.ca/HouseP-ublications/Publication.aspx?Do-cId=5524772.*
4) Canada, Parliament, House of Commons, Standing Committee on Procedure and House Affairs, *Evidence from the Subcommittee on Private Members' Business of the Standing Committee on Procedure and House Affairs*, 41st Parliament, 1st Session, Number 7 (March 21, 2013), *www.parl.gc.ca/HouseP-ublications/Publication.aspx?Do-cId=6055301&Language=E&-Mode=1&Parl=41&Ses=1.*

5. CABINET: A REPRESENTATIVE NOT A DELIBERATIVE BODY

1) "Harper cabinet rift emerges over Quebec secession rules," CBC News, October 21, 2013, accessed March 5, 2014, *www.cbc.ca/m/touch/cana-da/story/1.2131110.*
2) Ari Altstedter. "Jim Flaherty says Canada may see bigger surplus, but the loonie has further to fall," *Financial Post*, January 6, 2014, *http://business.financialpost.com/2014/01/06/jim-flaherty-says-canada-may-see-bigger-surplus-but-the-loonie-has-further-to-fall/.*

6. PARTY DISCIPLINE: YOU ARE THERE TO SUPPORT THE TEAM

1) Brent Rathgeber, "The Parliamentary Budget Officer; Time to Turn the Page," February 6, 2013, accessed March 5, 2014, *http://brentrathge-ber.ca/the-parliamentary-budget-of-ficer-time-to-turn-the-page/.*
2) Canada, Parliament, House of Commons, "Routine Proceedings: Privilege, Gordon O'Connor," *De-*

bates, 41st Parliament, 1st Session, vol. 146, no. 229, March 26, 2013, *www.parl.gc.ca/HousePublications/ Publication.aspx?Language=en&- Mode=1&DocId=6065804&File=.*

3) Andrew Coyne, "Rathgeber returns politics to normal, where conscience does not submit to power," *National Post*, June 7, 2013, *http://fullcom- ment.nationalpost.com/2013/06/07/ andrew-coyne-rathgeber-returns- politics-to-normal-where-conscience- does-not-submit-to-power/.*

4) P.J. O'Rourke, *Parliament of Whores: A Lone Humorist Attempts to Explain the Entire US Government* (New York: Grove Press, 2003).

7. THE PRIME MINISTER: THE AMERICANIZATION OF CANADIAN POLITICS

1) Russell, quoted in Andrew Coyne, "Canada, like U.S., hostage to political minority," Canada.com, October 9, 2013, accessed March 5, 2014, *http://o. canada.com/news/canada-like-u-s-hos- tage-to-political-minority/.*

2) Jim Travers, "An eloquent plea for democracy," *Toronto Star*, March 4, 2011, *www.thestar.com/news/cana- da/2011/03/04/an_eloquent_plea_ for_democracy.html.*

3) "Stephen Harper's most contro- versial quotes compiled — by Tories," *Toronto Star*, April 25, 2011, *www.thestar.com/news/ canada/2011/04/25/stephen_harp- ers_most_controversial_quotes_com- piled_by_tories.html.*

4) Bill C-559: An Act to amend the Canada Elections Act and the Parliament of Canada Act (reforms), (Canada, 41st Parl., 2nd sess.),

www.parl.gc.ca/HousePublications/ Publication.aspx?Language=E&- Mode=1&DocId=6360606.

8. THE PRIME MINISTER'S OFFICE: THE GANG THAT DOESN'T SHOOT STRAIGHT

1) Days after the 2006 general election, David Emerson, who was re-elected as a Liberal in Vancouver Kingsway, crossed the floor to join the Conser- vative caucus and cabinet.

9. POLITICAL PARTIES: POWER IS AN END IN ITSELF

1) "Members quit Anders' riding association," CBC News, February 11, 2010, accessed March 5, 2014, *www.cbc.ca/news/canada/calgary/ members-quit-anders-riding-associ- ation-1.871764.*

2) Bill C-377: An Act to amend the In- come Tax Act (requirements for labour organizations), (Canada, 41st Parl., 2nd sess.), *www.parl.gc.ca/HousePublica- tions/Publication.aspx?Language=E&- Mode=1&DocId=6256612.*

10. THE BUREAUCRACY: INFORMATION IS POWER

1) Canada, Parliament, House of Com- mons, Special Committee on the Canadian Mission in Afghanistan, "Evidence: Special Committee on the Canadian Mission in Afghanistan 18 November 2009," 40th Parliament, 2nd Session, Number 15 (November 18, 2009), *www.parl.gc.ca/House- Publications/Publication.aspx?Do- cId=4236267&Language=E&- Mode=1&Parl=40&Ses=2.*

2) "EI whistleblower suspended without pay," CBC News, July 20, 2013 (up-

dated July 22, 2013), accessed March 5, 2014, *www.cbc.ca/news/canada/british-columbia/ei-whistleblower-suspended-without-pay-1.1407761.*

3) Canada, Clerk of the Privy Council, "Modernizing the Employment Model," Seventh Report of the Prime Minister's Advisory Committee on the Public Service, Ottawa: Parliament of Canada, 2013, *www.clerk.gc.ca/eng/feature.asp?pageId=314.*

4) Emily Chung, "Muzzling of federal scientists widespread, survey suggests." CBC News, October 21, 2013 (updated 22 October 2013), accessed March 5, 2013, *www.cbc.ca/news/technology/muzzling-of-federal-scientists-widespread-survey-suggests-1.2128859.*

5) Public Servants Disclosure Protection Act, S.C. 2005, c.46, Government of Canada: Justice Laws, *http://laws-lois.justice.gc.ca/eng/acts/P-31.9/index.html.* The act is current to February 6, 2014, and was last amended on March 16, 2012.

6) Public Interest Disclosure (Whistleblower Protection) Act, Alberta, S.A., 2012, P-39.5, *www.qp.alberta.ca/documents/Acts/p39p5.pdf.*

7) The Association of Certified Fraud Examiners confirms that the most effective means of exposing fraud is tips from employees and anonymous sources (43 percent).

8) Association of Certified Fraud Examiners, "2012 Report to the Nations," accessed March 5, 2014, *www.acfe.com/rttn.aspx*

9) Canada, Office of the Parliamentary Budget Officer, "An Estimate of the Fiscal Impact of Canada's Proposed Acquisition of the F-35 Lightning II Joint Strike Fighter," Ottawa: Office of the Parliamentary Budget Officer, 2011, *www.pbo-dpb.gc.ca/files/files/Publications/F-35_Cost_Estimate_EN.pdf.*

10) Parliament of Canada Act, c. P-1, s. 79.3, R.S.C., 1985, Government of Canada: Justice Laws, *http://laws-lois.justice.gc.ca/eng/acts/P-1/FullText.html.*

11) "Sonia L'Heureux, New PBO, Says Tory Government Not Sharing Information," *Huffington Post*, July 22, 2013, accessed March 5, 2014, *www.huffingtonpost.ca/2013/07/22/new-pbo-says-two-requests_n_3636216.html.*

11. WITHHOLDING THE POWER: CANADA'S BROKEN ACCESS TO INFORMATION LAWS

1) Access to Information Act, Government of Canada: Justice Laws, *http://laws-lois.justice.gc.ca/eng/acts/a-1/FullText.html.*

2) Canadian Press, "Free-speech report takes aim at Harper government's 'culture of secrecy,'" *Macleans*, May 3, 2013, *www2.macleans.ca/2013/05/03/free-speech-report-takes-aim-at-harper-governments-culture-of-secrecy-2/.*

3) John Reid. "The Future of Accountability — The Federal Government's Accountability Act and Discussion Paper and the Open Government Act," 2006 Access and Privacy Appreciation Dinner, University of Alberta, Edmonton, Alberta, June 2006.

4) *Ibid*

5) Canada, Parliament, House of

Commons, Standing Committee on Access to Information Privacy and Ethics, "The *Access to Information Act*: First Steps Towards Renewal," 40th Parliament, 2nd Session, June 2009, *www.parl.gc.ca/content/hoc/Committee/402/ETHI/Reports/RP3999593/ethirp11/ethirp11-e.pdf*.

6) Canada, Office of the Information Commissioner of Canada, "The Access to Information Act in Canada: Taking Stock of 30 years." by Suzanne Legault, Ottawa: Office of the Information Commissioner of Canada, December 5, 2013, *www.oic-ci.gc.ca/eng/media-room-salle-media_speeches-discours_2013_9.aspx*.

7) Canada, Office of the Information Commissioner of Canada, "Speaking Notes of Suzanne Legault, Information Commissioner of Canada, to the Canadian Legal Information Institute (CanLII) Conference," by Suzanne Legault, Ottawa: Office of the Information Commissioner of Canada, 2013, accessed March 5, 2014, *www.oic-ci.gc.ca/eng/media-room-salle-media_speeches-discours_2013_5.aspx*.

8) Bob Carty, "Access Denied!" *CJFE Review of Free Expression in Canada* (2014): 27.

9) R. Gary Dickson, Letter to Suzanne Legault, February 8, 2013, Office of the Information and Privacy Commissioner of Saskatchewan, accessed March 5, 2014, *www.oipc.sk.ca/What's%20New/Letter%20to%20Suzanne%20Legault%20-%20Consultation%20on%20the%20Access%20to%20Information%20Act.pdf*.

10) Justice Louis D. Brandeis, "Louis D. Brandeis Quotes," Brandeis University, accessed March 5, 2014, *www.brandeis.edu/legacyfund/bio.html*.

11) Dickson, Letter.

12. THE MEDIA: IF IT BLEEDS, IT LEADS

1) For a less favourable account, see Graeme Smith, *The Dogs are Eating them Now: Our War in Afghanistan* (Toronto: Knopf Canada, 2013).

13. JUDICIAL REVIEW: A TRUE CHECK ON GOVERNMENT POWER

1) Canada, Supreme Court of Canada, "Canada (Attorney General) v. Bedford," *Judgments of the Supreme Court of Canada*, *http://scc-csc.lexum.com/scc-csc/scc-csc/en/item/13389/index.do*.

2) Canada, Department of Justice, "Statement by the Minister of Justice Regarding the Supreme Court of Canada Ruling in Attorney General of Canada v. Bedford *et al.*," *www.justice.gc.ca/eng/news-nouv/nr-cp/2013/doc_33020.html*.

3) David Akin. "What really bugs Conservatives about the Supreme Court prostitution ruling," Canoe.ca News, December 20, 2013, accessed March 5, 2014, *http://blogs.canoe.ca/davidakin/politics/what-really-bugs-conservatives-about-the-supreme-court-prostitution-ruling/comment-page-1/*.

4) Apparently it is not illegal to sell a human organ in Canada but it is illegal to buy one.

5) Canada, Supreme Court of Canada, "R. v. Morgentaler," *Judgments of the Supreme Court of Canada*, *http://scc-csc.lexum.com/scc-csc/scc-csc/en/item/288/index.do*.

6) Canada, Supreme Court of Canada, "Vriend v. Alberta," Judgments of the Supreme Court of Canada,